# CATULLUS

## ADVANCED PLACEMENT EDITION

Teacher's Manual

Reproducible Pages

*by*

**Henry V. Bender, Ph.D.**
St. Joseph's Preparatory School and Villanova University

*and*

**Phyllis Young Forsyth, Ph.D.**
University of Waterloo

Bolchazy-Carducci Publishers, Inc.
1997

*Contributing editor:*
**Thalia Pantelidis Hocker**

*General editor:*
**Laurie Haight**

*Cover illustration:*
Girl with pigeons, fifth century B.C.
Athenian grave stele, Metropolitan Museum, New York

*Cover design:*
**Bensen Studios**

© 1996 Bolchazy-Carducci Publishers, Inc.

# Bolchazy-Carducci Publishers, Inc.
1000 Brown Street, Unit 101
Wauconda, Illinois 60084

Printed in the United States of America
**1997**

ISBN 0-86516-276-X

# Contents

Preface .................................................................................................. 1

Text of Poems ..................................................................................... 3

Translation of Poems ...................................................................... 49

A. P. Tests .......................................................................................... 61

Bibliography ..................................................................................... 89

Catullan Poems in English ............................................................ 95

# Preface

This manual provides a complete Latin text of the poems of Catullus which comprise the A. P. syllabus so that teachers may make overhead transparencies for classroom use. This is particularly valuable when reviewing or testing a poem in class. The manual also offers a working translation of each poem. These translations have several practical applications for the students. They may be used for review, to supplement the basic process of mastery of the text. They are useful to compare with the student's first efforts at translation. They are also of value when set against fine, polished translations which have been done by various authors.

A full series of tests is also included. These are keyed in sequence to sets of poems which in my experience seem best when handled as a unit. But testing times, emphases, and syntactical terms vary greatly from program to program. So at the very least, these tests may serve as worthwhile homework, or may provide a base which can be adjusted to the evaluation needs of individual classes. The essay portions reflect some of my own questions as well as those drawn from and adapted to the language and structure of the free response sections of the A. P. Examination. Finally, a select bibliography is attached.

I wish to express my personal thanks to Bolchazy-Carducci Publishers, particularly to Dr. Ladislaus Bolchazy for his support and encourage-ment, and to Thalia Hocker for her creative suggestions in formatting the text. I am most deeply grateful to my co-author, Professor Phyllis Young Forsyth of the University of Waterloo, for her meticulous and thorough work on this manuscript. Her many suggestions and revisions were simply indispensable.

It is the hope of the authors, editors, and publisher that this text may facilitate the considerably difficult task facing the teacher who brings A. P. to the Latin classroom.

Henry V. Bender, Ph.D.<br>
St. Joseph's Preparatory School<br>
and Villanova University<br>
Philadelphia, PA<br>
August, 1996

# 1

Cui dono lepidum novum libellum
arida modo pumice expolitum?
Corneli, tibi: namque tu solebas
meas esse aliquid putare nugas
iam tum, cum ausus es unus Italorum     5
omne aevum tribus explicare cartis
doctis, Iuppiter, et laboriosis.
quare habe tibi quidquid hoc libelli
qualecumque; quod, <o> patrona virgo,
plus uno maneat perenne saeclo.     10

## 2

Passer, deliciae meae puellae,

quicum ludere, quem in sinu tenere,

cui primum digitum dare appetenti

et acris solet incitare morsus,

cum desiderio meo nitenti 5

carum nescio quid lubet iocari,

et solaciolum sui doloris,

credo, ut tum gravis acquiescat ardor:

tecum ludere sicut ipsa possem

et tristis animi levare curas! 10

## 2B

tam gratum est mihi quam ferunt puellae

pernici aureolum fuisse malum,

quod zonam soluit diu ligatam.

## 3

Lugete, O Veneres Cupidinesque,
et quantum est hominum venustiorum:
passer mortuus est meae puellae,
passer, deliciae meae puellae,
quem plus illa oculis suis amabat. 5
nam mellitus erat suamque norat
ipsam tam bene quam puella matrem,
nec sese a gremio illius movebat,
sed circumsiliens modo huc modo illuc
ad solam dominam usque pipiabat; 10
qui nunc it per iter tenebricosum
illud, unde negant redire quemquam.
at vobis male sit, malae tenebrae
Orci, quae omnia bella devoratis:
tam bellum mihi passerem abstulistis. 15
O factum male!  O miselle passer!
tua nunc opera meae puellae
flendo turgiduli rubent ocelli.

## 4

Phaselus ille, quem videtis, hospites,
ait fuisse navium celerrimus,
neque ullius natantis impetum trabis
nequisse praeterire, sive palmulis
opus foret volare sive linteo. 5
et hoc negat minacis Hadriatici
negare litus insulasve Cycladas
Rhodumque nobilem horridamque Thraciam
Propontida trucemve Ponticum sinum,
ubi iste post phaselus antea fuit 10
comata silva; nam Cytorio in iugo
loquente saepe sibilum edidit coma.
Amastri Pontica et Cytore buxifer,
tibi haec fuisse et esse cognitissima
ait phaselus: ultima ex origine 15
tuo stetisse dicit in cacumine,
tuo imbuisse palmulas in aequore,
et inde tot per impotentia freta
erum tulisse, laeva sive dextera
vocaret aura, sive utrumque Iuppiter 20
simul secundus incidisset in pedem;
neque ulla vota litoralibus deis
sibi esse facta, cum veniret a mari
novissimo hunc ad usque limpidum lacum.
sed haec prius fuere: nunc recondita 25
senet quiete seque dedicat tibi,
gemelle Castor et gemelle Castoris.

## 5

Vivamus, mea Lesbia, atque amemus,
rumoresque senum severiorum
omnes unius aestimemus assis!
soles occidere et redire possunt:
nobis cum semel occidit brevis lux,      5
nox est perpetua una dormienda.
da mi basia mille, deinde centum,
dein mille altera, dein secunda centum,
deinde usque altera mille, deinde centum.
dein, cum milia multa fecerimus,      10
conturbabimus illa, ne sciamus,
aut ne quis malus invidere possit,
cum tantum sciat esse basiorum.

## 7

Quaeris, quot mihi basiationes

tuae, Lesbia, sint satis superque.

quam magnus numerus Libyssae harenae

lasarpiciferis iacet Cyrenis

oraclum Iovis inter aestuosi 5

et Batti veteris sacrum sepulcrum;

aut quam sidera multa, cum tacet nox,

furtivos hominum vident amores:

tam te basia multa basiare

vesano satis et super Catullo est, 10

quae nec pernumerare curiosi

possint nec mala fascinare lingua.

## 8

Miser Catulle, desinas ineptire,
et quod vides perisse perditum ducas.
fulsere quondam candidi tibi soles,
cum ventitabas quo puella ducebat
amata nobis quantum amabitur nulla. 5
ibi illa multa cum iocosa fiebant,
quae tu volebas nec puella nolebat,
fulsere vere candidi tibi soles.
nunc iam illa non volt: tu quoque inpote\<ns noli\>,
nec quae fugit sectare, nec miser vive, 10
sed obstinata mente perfer, obdura.
vale, puella. iam Catullus obdurat,
nec te requiret nec rogabit invitam.
at tu dolebis, cum rogaberis nulla.
scelesta, vae te! quae tibi manet vita? 15
quis nunc te adibit? cui videberis bella?
quem nunc amabis? cuius esse diceris?
quem basiabis? cui labella mordebis?
at tu, Catulle, destinatus obdura.

## 9

Verani, omnibus e meis amicis
antistans mihi milibus trecentis,
venistine domum ad tuos penates
fratresque unanimos anumque matrem?
venisti. O mihi nuntii beati! 5
visam te incolumem audiamque Hiberum
narrantem loca, facta, nationes,
ut mos est tuus, applicansque collum
iucundum os oculosque suaviabor.
O quantum est hominum beatiorum, 10
quid me laetius est beatiusve?

## 10

Varus me meus ad suos amores
visum duxerat e foro otiosum,
scortillum, ut mihi tum repente visum est,
non sane illepidum neque invenustum.
huc ut venimus, incidere nobis 5
sermones varii, in quibus, quid esset
iam Bithynia, quo modo se haberet,
et quonam mihi profuisset aere.
respondi id quod erat, nihil neque ipsis
nec praetoribus esse nec cohorti, 10
cur quisquam caput unctius referret,
praesertim quibus esset irrumator
praetor, nec faceret pili cohortem.
'at certe tamen,' inquiunt 'quod illic
natum dicitur esse, comparasti 15
ad lecticam homines.' ego, ut puellae
unum me facerem beatiorem,
'non' inquam 'mihi tam fuit maligne,
ut, provincia quod mala incidisset,
non possem octo homines parare rectos.' 20
at mi nullus erat nec hic neque illic,
fractum qui veteris pedem grabati
in collo sibi collocare posset.
hic illa, ut decuit cinaediorem,
'quaeso,' inquit 'mihi, mi Catulle, paulum 25
istos commoda: nam volo ad Serapim
deferri.' 'mane,' inquii puellae,
'istud quod modo dixeram me habere,
fugit me ratio: meus sodalis—
Cinna est Gaius,—is sibi paravit. 30
verum, utrum illius an mei, quid ad me?
utor tam bene quam mihi pararim.
sed tu insulsa male et molesta vivis,
per quam non licet esse neglegentem.'

## 11

Furi et Aureli, comites Catulli,
sive in extremos penetrabit Indos,
litus ut longe resonante Eoa
    tunditur unda,
sive in Hyrcanos Arabasve molles,     5
seu Sagas sagittiferosve Parthos,
sive quae septemgeminus colorat
    aequora Nilus,
sive trans altas gradietur Alpes,
Caesaris visens monimenta magni,     10
Gallicum Rhenum, horribile aequor ulti-
    mosque Britannos,
omnia haec, quaecumque feret voluntas
caelitum, temptare simul parati,
pauca nuntiate meae puellae     15
    non bona dicta.
cum suis vivat valeatque moechis,
quos simul complexa tenet trecentos,
nullum amans vere, sed identidem omnium
    ilia rumpens;     20
nec meum respectet, ut ante, amorem,
qui illius culpa cecidit velut prati
ultimi flos, praetereunte postquam
    tactus aratro est.

## 12

Marrucine Asini, manu sinistra
non belle uteris: in ioco atque vino
tollis lintea neglegentiorum.
hoc salsum esse putas? fugit te, inepte:
quamvis sordida res et invenusta est.　　　5
non credis mihi? crede Pollioni
fratri, qui tua furta vel talento
mutari velit: est enim leporum
differtus puer ac facetiarum.
quare aut hendecasyllabos trecentos　　　10
exspecta, aut mihi linteum remitte,
quod me non movet aestimatione,
verum est mnemosynum mei sodalis.
nam sudaria Saetaba ex Hiberis
miserunt mihi muneri Fabullus　　　15
et Veranius: haec amem necesse est
ut Veraniolum meum et Fabullum.

## 13

Cenabis bene, mi Fabulle, apud me
paucis, si tibi di favent, diebus,
si tecum attuleris bonam atque magnam
cenam, non sine candida puella
et vino et sale et omnibus cachinnis.  5
haec si, inquam, attuleris, venuste noster,
cenabis bene; nam tui Catulli
plenus sacculus est aranearum.
sed contra accipies meros amores
seu quid suavius elegantiusve est:  10
nam unguentum dabo, quod meae puellae
donarunt Veneres Cupidinesque,
quod tu cum olfacies, deos rogabis,
totum ut te faciant, Fabulle, nasum.

## 22

Suffenus iste, Vare, quem probe nosti,
homo est venustus et dicax et urbanus,
idemque longe plurimos facit versus.
puto esse ego illi milia aut decem aut plura
perscripta, nec sic ut fit in palimpseston     5
relata: cartae regiae, novi libri,
novi umbilici, lora rubra membranae,
derecta plumbo et pumice omnia aequata.
haec cum legas tu, bellus ille et urbanus
Suffenus unus caprimulgus aut fossor     10
rursus videtur: tantum abhorret ac mutat.
hoc quid putemus esse? qui modo scurra
aut si quid hac re scitius videbatur,
idem infaceto est infacetior rure,
simul poemata attigit, neque idem umquam     15
aeque est beatus ac poema cum scribit:
tam gaudet in se tamque se ipse miratur.
nimirum idem omnes fallimur, neque est quisquam
quem non in aliqua re videre Suffenum
possis. suus cuique attributus est error;     20
sed non videmus manticae quod in tergo est.

## 27

Minister vetuli puer Falerni,

inger mi calices amariores,

ut lex Postumiae iubet magistrae

ebrioso acino ebriosioris.

at vos quo lubet hinc abite, lymphae,     5

vini pernicies, et ad severos

migrate.  hic merus est Thyonianus.

## 31

Paene insularum, Sirmio, insularumque
ocelle, quascumque in liquentibus stagnis
marique vasto fert uterque Neptunus,
quam te libenter quamque laetus inviso,
vix mi ipse credens Thuniam atque Bithunos     5
liquisse campos et videre te in tuto.
O quid solutis est beatius curis,
cum mens onus reponit, ac peregrino
labore fessi venimus larem ad nostrum,
desideratoque acquiescimus lecto?              10
hoc est quod unum est pro laboribus tantis.
salve, O venusta Sirmio, atque ero gaude
gaudente, vosque, O Lydiae lacus undae,
ridete quidquid est domi cachinnorum.

## 34

Dianae sumus in fide
puellae et pueri integri:
&lt;Dianam pueri integri&gt;
 puellaeque canamus.

O Latonia, maximi 5
magna progenies Iovis,
quam mater prope Deliam
deposivit olivam,

montium domina ut fores
silvarumque virentium 10
saltuumque reconditorum
amniumque sonantum:

tu Lucina dolentibus
Iuno dicta puerperis,
tu potens Trivia et notho es 15
dicta lumine Luna.

tu cursu, dea, menstruo
metiens iter annuum,
rustica agricolae bonis
tecta frugibus exples. 20

sis quocumque tibi placet
sancta nomine, Romulique,
antique ut solita es, bona
sospites ope gentem.

## 35

Poetae tenero, meo sodali,
velim Caecilio, papyre, dicas
Veronam veniat, Novi relinquens
Comi moenia Lariumque litus.
nam quasdam volo cogitationes 5
amici accipiat sui meique.
quare, si sapiet, viam vorabit,
quamvis candida milies puella
euntem revocet, manusque collo
ambas iniciens roget morari. 10
quae nunc, si mihi vera nuntiantur,
illum deperit impotente amore.
nam quo tempore legit incohatam
Dindymi dominam, ex eo misellae
ignes interiorem edunt medullam. 15
ignosco tibi, Sapphica puella
musa doctior; est enim venuste
Magna Caecilio incohata Mater.

## 36

Annales Volusi, cacata carta,
votum solvite pro mea puella.
nam sanctae Veneri Cupidinique
vovit, si sibi restitutus essem
desissemque truces vibrare iambos, 5
electissima pessimi poetae
scripta tardipedi deo daturam
infelicibus ustulanda lignis.
et hoc pessima se puella vidit
iocose lepide vovere divis. 10
nunc o caeruleo creata ponto,
quae sanctum Idalium Uriosque apertos
quaeque Ancona Cnidumque harundinosam
colis quaeque Amathunta quaeque Golgos
quaeque Durrachium Hadriae tabernam, 15
acceptum face redditumque votum,
si non illepidum neque invenustum est.
at vos interea venite in ignem,
pleni ruris et inficetiarum
annales Volusi, cacata carta. 20

## 43

Salve, nec minimo puella naso
nec bello pede nec nigris ocellis
nec longis digitis nec ore sicco
nec sane nimis elegante lingua,
decoctoris amica Formiani. 5
ten provincia narrat esse bellam?
tecum Lesbia nostra comparatur?
O saeclum insapiens et infacetum!

## 44

O funde noster seu Sabine seu Tiburs
(nam te esse Tiburtem autumant, quibus
    non est
cordi Catullum laedere; at quibus cordi est,
quovis Sabinum pignore esse contendunt),
sed seu Sabine sive verius Tiburs,         5
fui libenter in tua suburbana
villa, malamque pectore expuli tussim,
non immerenti quam mihi meus venter,
dum sumptuosas appeto, dedit, cenas.
nam, Sestianus dum volo esse conviva,         10
orationem in Antium petitorem
plenam veneni et pestilentiae legi.
hic me gravedo frigida et frequens tussis
quassavit usque, dum in tuum sinum fugi,
et me recuravi otioque et urtica.         15
quare refectus maximas tibi grates
ago, meum quod non es ulta peccatum.
nec deprecor iam, si nefaria scripta
Sesti recepso, quin gravedinem et tussim
non mi, sed ipsi Sestio ferat frigus,         20
qui tunc vocat me, cum malum librum legi.

## 45

Acmen Septimius suos amores
tenens in gremio 'mea' inquit 'Acme,
ni te perdite amo atque amare porro
omnes sum assidue paratus annos,
quantum qui pote plurimum perire, 5
solus in Libya Indiaque tosta
caesio veniam obvius leoni.'
hoc ut dixit, Amor sinistra ut ante
dextra sternuit approbationem.
at Acme leviter caput reflectens 10
et dulcis pueri ebrios ocellos
illo purpureo ore suaviata,
'sic,' inquit 'mea vita Septimille,
huic uni domino usque serviamus,
ut multo mihi maior acriorque 15
ignis mollibus ardet in medullis.'
hoc ut dixit, Amor sinistra ut ante
dextra sternuit approbationem.
nunc ab auspicio bono profecti
mutuis animis amant amantur. 20
unam Septimius misellus Acmen
mavult quam Syrias Britanniasque:
uno in Septimio fidelis Acme
facit delicias libidinesque.
quis ullos homines beatiores 25
vidit, quis Venerem auspicatiorem?

## 46

Iam ver egelidos refert tepores,
iam caeli furor aequinoctialis
iucundis Zephyri silescit aureis.
linquantur Phrygii, Catulle, campi
Nicaeaeque ager uber aestuosae:　　　5
ad claras Asiae volemus urbes.
iam mens praetrepidans avet vagari,
iam laeti studio pedes vigescunt.
O dulces comitum valete coetus,
longe quos simul a domo profectos　　　10
diversae varie viae reportant.

## 49

Disertissime Romuli nepotum,

quot sunt quotque fuere, Marce Tulli,

quotque post aliis erunt in annis,

gratias tibi maximas Catullus

agit pessimus omnium poeta, 5

tanto pessimus omnium poeta,

quanto tu optimus omnium patronus.

## 50

Hesterno, Licini, die otiosi
multum lusimus in meis tabellis,
ut convenerat esse delicatos:
scribens versiculos uterque nostrum
ludebat numero modo hoc modo illoc, 5
reddens mutua per iocum atque vinum.
atque illinc abii tuo lepore
incensus, Licini, facetiisque,
ut nec me miserum cibus iuvaret
nec somnus tegeret quiete ocellos, 10
sed toto indomitus furore lecto
versarer, cupiens videre lucem,
ut tecum loquerer simulque ut essem.
at defessa labore membra postquam
semimortua lectulo iacebant, 15
hoc, iucunde, tibi poema feci,
ex quo perspiceres meum dolorem.
nunc audax cave sis, precesque nostras,
oramus, cave despuas, ocelle,
ne poenas Nemesis reposcat a te. 20
est vemens dea: laedere hanc caveto.

# 51

Ille mi par esse deo videtur,
ille, si fas est, superare divos,
qui sedens adversus identidem te
    spectat et audit

dulce ridentem, misero quod omnis      5
eripit sensus mihi: nam simul te,
Lesbia, aspexi, nihil est super mi
    * * * * * * * * * * * *

lingua sed torpet, tenuis sub artus
flamma demanat, sonitu suopte      10
tintinant aures, gemina teguntur
    lumina nocte.

otium, Catulle, tibi molestum est:
otio exsultas nimiumque gestis:
otium et reges prius et beatas      15
    perdidit urbes.

## 53

Risi nescio quem modo e corona,
qui, cum mirifice Vatiniana
meus crimina Calvos explicasset,
admirans ait haec manusque tollens,
'di magni, salaputium disertum!'       5

# 62

Vesper adest, iuvenes, consurgite: Vesper Olympo
exspectata diu vix tandem lumina tollit.
surgere iam tempus, iam pinguis linquere mensas,
iam veniet virgo, iam dicetur hymenaeus.
Hymen O Hymenaee, Hymen ades O Hymenaee!     5

Cernitis, innuptae, iuvenes? consurgite contra;
nimirum Oetaeos ostendit Noctifer ignes.
sic certest; viden ut perniciter exsiluere?
non temere exsiluere, canent quod vincere par est.
Hymen O Hymenaee, Hymen ades O Hymenaee!     10

Non facilis nobis, aequales, palma parata est;
aspicite, innuptae secum ut meditata requirunt.
non frustra meditantur: habent memorabile quod sit;
nec mirum, penitus quae tota mente laborant.
nos alio mentes, alio divisimus aures;     15
iure igitur vincemur: amat victoria curam.
quare nunc animos saltem convertite vestros;
dicere iam incipient, iam respondere decebit.
Hymen O Hymenaee, Hymen ades O Hymenaee!

Hespere, quis caelo fertur crudelior ignis?     20
qui natam possis complexu avellere matris,
complexu matris retinentem avellere natam,
et iuveni ardenti castam donare puellam.
quid faciunt hostes capta crudelius urbe?
Hymen O Hymenaee, Hymen ades O Hymenaee!     25

Hespere, quis caelo lucet iucundior ignis?
qui desponsa tua firmes conubia flamma,
quae pepigere viri, pepigerunt ante parentes,
nec iunxere prius quam se tuus extulit ardor.
quid datur a divis felici optatius hora? 30
Hymen O Hymenaee, Hymen ades O Hymenaee!

Hesperus e nobis, aequales, abstulit unam.
* * * * * * * * * * * * * * * * * * * *
* * * * * * * * * * * * * * * * * * * *
namque tuo adventu vigilat custodia semper,
nocte latent fures, quos idem saepe revertens,
Hespere, mutato comprendis nomine Eous. 35
at lubet innuptis ficto te carpere questu.
quid tum, si carpunt, tacita quem mente requirunt?
Hymen O Hymenaee, Hymen ades O Hymenaee!

Ut flos in saeptis secretus nascitur hortis,
ignotus pecori, nullo convolsus aratro, 40
quem mulcent aurae, firmat sol, educat imber;
multi illum pueri, multae optavere puellae:
idem cum tenui carptus defloruit ungui,
nulli illum pueri, nullae optavere puellae:
sic virgo, dum intacta manet, dum cara suis est; 45
cum castum amisit polluto corpore florem,
nec pueris iucunda manet, nec cara puellis.
Hymen O Hymenaee, Hymen ades O Hymenaee!

Ut vidua in nudo vitis quae nascitur arvo,
numquam se extollit, numquam mitem educat
    uvam, 50
sed tenerum prono deflectens pondere corpus
iam iam contingit summum radice flagellum;
hanc nulli agricolae, nulli coluere iuvenci:
at si forte eadem est ulmo coniuncta marito,
multi illam agricolae, multi coluere iuvenci: 55
sic virgo, dum intacta manet, dum inculta senescit;
cum par conubium maturo tempore adepta est,
cara viro magis et minus est invisa parenti.
<Hymen O Hymenaee, Hymen ades
    O Hymenaee!> 58b

Et tu ne pugna cum tali coniuge, virgo.
non aequom est pugnare, pater cui tradidit
    ipse, 60
ipse pater cum matre, quibus parere necesse est.
virginitas non tota tua est, ex parte parentum est,
tertia pars patrist, pars est data tertia matri,
tertia sola tua est: noli pugnare duobus,
qui genero sua iura simul cum dote dederunt. 65
Hymen O Hymenaee, Hymen ades O Hymenaee!

## 70

Nulli se dicit mulier mea nubere malle
    quam mihi, non si se Iuppiter ipse petat.
dicit: sed mulier cupido quod dicit amanti,
    in vento et rapida scribere oportet aqua.

## 72

Dicebas quondam solum te nosse Catullum,
  Lesbia, nec prae me velle tenere Iovem.
dilexi tum te non tantum ut vulgus amicam,
  sed pater ut gnatos diligit et generos.
nunc te cognovi: quare etsi impensius uror,     5
  multo mi tamen es vilior et levior.
qui potis est, inquis? quod amantem iniuria talis
  cogit amare magis, sed bene velle minus.

## 73

Desine de quoquam quicquam bene velle mereri
   aut aliquem fieri posse putare pium.
omnia sunt ingrata, nihil fecisse benigne
   <prodest,> immo etiam taedet obestque magis;
ut mihi, quem nemo gravius nec acerbius urget, 5
   quam modo qui me unum atque unicum amicum
      habuit.

## 75

Huc est mens deducta tua mea, Lesbia, culpa
atque ita se officio perdidit ipsa suo,
ut iam nec bene velle queat tibi, si optima fias,
nec desistere amare, omnia si facias.

## 76

Siqua recordanti benefacta priora voluptas
    est homini, cum se cogitat esse pium,
nec sanctam violasse fidem, nec foedere nullo
    divum ad fallendos numine abusum homines,
multa parata manent in longa aetate, Catulle,         5
    ex hoc ingrato gaudia amore tibi.
nam quaecumque homines bene cuiquam aut dicere possunt
    aut facere, haec a te dictaque factaque sunt.
omnia quae ingratae perierunt credita menti.
    quare iam te cur amplius excrucies?         10
quin tu animo offirmas atque istinc teque reducis,
    et dis invitis desinis esse miser?
difficile est longum subito deponere amorem,
    difficile est, verum hoc qua lubet efficias:
una salus haec est, hoc est tibi pervincendum,         15
    hoc facias, sive id non pote sive pote.
O di, si vestrum est misereri, aut si quibus umquam
    extremam iam ipsa in morte tulistis opem,
me miserum aspicite et, si vitam puriter egi,
    eripite hanc pestem perniciemque mihi,         20
quae mihi subrepens imos ut torpor in artus
    expulit ex omni pectore laetitias.
non iam illud quaero, contra me ut diligat illa,
    aut, quod non potis est, esse pudica velit:
ipse valere opto et taetrum hunc deponere morbum.         25
    O di, reddite mi hoc pro pietate mea.

## 77

Rufe mihi frustra ac nequiquam credite amice
    (frustra? immo magno cum pretio atque malo),
sicine subrepsti mi, atque intestina perurens
    ei misero eripuisti omnia nostra bona?
eripuisti, heu heu nostrae crudele venenum     5
    vitae, heu heu nostrae pestis amicitiae.

## 83

Lesbia mi praesente viro mala plurima dicit:
   haec illi fatuo maxima laetitia est.
mule, nihil sentis? si nostri oblita taceret,
   sana esset: nunc quod gannit et obloquitur,
non solum meminit, sed, quae multo acrior est res,    5
   irata est. hoc est, uritur et loquitur.

## 84

Chommoda dicebat, si quando commoda vellet
    dicere, et insidias Arrius hinsidias,
et tum mirifice sperabat se esse locutum,
    cum quantum poterat dixerat hinsidias.
credo, sic mater, sic liber avunculus eius,     5
    sic maternus avus dixerat atque avia.
hoc misso in Syriam requierant omnibus aures:
    audibant eadem haec leniter et leviter,
nec sibi postilla metuebant talia verba,
    cum subito affertur nuntius horribilis,     10
Ionios fluctus, postquam illuc Arrius isset,
    iam non Ionios esse sed Hionios.

## 85

Odi et amo. quare id faciam, fortasse requiris?
nescio, sed fieri sentio et excrucior.

## 86

Quintia formosa est multis. mihi candida, longa,
　　recta est: haec ego sic singula confiteor.
totum illud formosa nego: nam nulla venustas,
　　nulla in tam magno est corpore mica salis.
Lesbia formosa est, quae cum pulcherrima tota est,     5
　　tum omnibus una omnis surripuit Veneres.

## 87

Nulla potest mulier tantum se dicere amatam
   vere, quantum a me Lesbia amata mea est.
nulla fides ullo fuit umquam foedere tanta,
   quanta in amore tuo ex parte reperta mea est.

## 92

Lesbia mi dicit semper male nec tacet umquam
    de me: Lesbia me dispeream nisi amat.
quo signo? quia sunt totidem mea: deprecor illam
    assidue, verum dispeream nisi amo.

## 95

Zmyrna mei Cinnae nonam post denique messem
   quam coepta est nonamque edita post hiemem,
milia cum interea quingenta Hortensius uno
   * * * * * * * * * * * * * * * * * * * * * *
Zmyrna cavas Satrachi penitus mittetur ad
        undas,      5
   Zmyrnam cana diu saecula pervolvent.
at Volusi annales Paduam morientur ad ipsam
   et laxas scombris saepe dabunt tunicas.

## 95B

Parva mei mihi sint cordi monimenta . . . ,
   at populus tumido gaudeat Antimacho.

## 96

Si quicquam mutis gratum acceptumve sepulcris
    accidere a nostro, Calve, dolore potest,
quo desiderio veteres renovamus amores
    atque olim missas flemus amicitias,
certe non tanto mors immatura dolori est         5
    Quintiliae, quantum gaudet amore tuo.

## 101

Multas per gentes et multa per aequora vectus
    advenio has miseras, frater, ad inferias,
ut te postremo donarem munere mortis
    et mutam nequiquam alloquerer cinerem.
quandoquidem fortuna mihi tete abstulit ipsum,     5
    heu miser indigne frater adempte mihi,
nunc tamen interea haec, prisco quae more parentum
    tradita sunt tristi munere ad inferias,
accipe fraterno multum manantia fletu,
    atque in perpetuum, frater, ave atque vale.     10

## 107

Si quicquam cupido optantique obtigit umquam
    insperanti, hoc est gratum animo proprie.
quare hoc est gratum †nobis quoque† carius auro
    quod te restituis, Lesbia, mi cupido.
restituis cupido atque insperanti, ipsa refers te         5
    nobis.  O lucem candidiore nota!
quis me uno vivit felicior, aut magis †hac est
    †optandus vita dicere quis poterit?

## 109

Iucundum, mea vita, mihi proponis amorem
    hunc nostrum inter nos perpetuumque fore.
di magni, facite ut vere promittere possit,
    atque id sincere dicat et ex animo,
ut liceat nobis tota perducere vita           5
    aeternum hoc sanctae foedus amicitiae.

# Translation of Poems

## ⇥ 1 ⇤

To whom am I giving this charming, new, little book freshly polished with dry pumice? To you, Cornelius: for you were accustomed to think that my nothings were something, already from the time when you, the only one of the Italians, dared to set forth all history in three scrolls, by Jupiter, learned and crafted! Therefore have for yourself whatever and whatever sort this little book may be; O patron Lady, let it remain enduring more than one generation.

## ⇥ 2 ⇤

Sparrow, delight of my girl, with whom she is accustomed to play, whom she is accustomed to hold in her lap, to whom, seeking it, she is accustomed to give her forefinger, and she is accustomed to stir up fierce bitings, when it pleases her, shining with desire for me, to make some pleasant joke, a consolation for her sadness, I think, so that then her heavy passion might subside: just as she herself does, I wish I could be able to play with you and to lighten the sad cares of my mind.

## ⇥ 2B ⇤

It is as pleasing to me as they say the golden apple was to that swift girl, (the apple) which freed up a girdle tied tight too long.

## ⇥ 3 ⇤

Mourn, you Venuses and Cupids, and however much of rather charming humankind there is: my girl's sparrow is dead, the sparrow, my girl's delight, which she loved more than her own eyes. For he was honey sweet and knew his own mistress as well as a girl (knew) her mother; nor did he move himself from her lap but, hopping now here now there, he piped up for his mistress only; (that sparrow) who now goes through the dark journey, that one from which they say no one ever returns. May it go badly for you, bad shadows of Orcus, who devour all pretty things: you have stolen from me such a beautiful sparrow. O what a bad deed! O the poor little sparrow! The eyes of my girlfriend are red and swollen with crying because of your deed.

## ⇥ 4 ⇤

That ship which you see, my friends, says that he is the fastest of ships and is not unable to surpass the attack-speed of any floating vessel, whether there is need to fly by oars or sail. Nor does he say that he does not know the shore of the threatening Adriatic or the Cyclades Islands, and noble Rhodes, and horrid Thracian Propontis or the destructive Pontic bay, where that afterwards-a-ship was before a leafy forest; for on the Cytorian ridge he often gave forth a sound from his talking foliage. O Pontic Amastris and boxwood-bearing Cytorus, the ship says that these things have been and are very well known to you: from his first beginning he says that he has stood on your ridge and has dipped his little oars in your sea, and from there has carried his master through so many uncontrollable straits, whether the breeze summons on the left or on the right, whether a favorable wind might have fallen at the same time on each foot of the sail; he says that no prayers for himself were made to the shore deities, when he came from the nearest sea to this serene lake. But these things have been before: now he grows old in hidden quiet and dedicates himself to you, twin Castor and twin of Castor.

## ⟞ 5 ⟝

Let us live and let us love, my Lesbia, and let us value all the rumors of the conservative old men as worth one penny! The suns can set and rise: as soon as the brief light of day sets for us, there is one never-ending night for sleeping. Give me a thousand kisses, then a hundred, then another thousand, then a second hundred, then another thousand, then a hundred; then when we shall have made many thousands, we will confuse them, lest we know, or lest any evil person be able to cast an evil eye, since he would know how many kisses there were.

## ⟞ 7 ⟝

You ask how many of your kisses, O Lesbia, are enough and more than enough for me. As great as is the quantity of sand in the Libyan desert of exotic Cyrene between the oracle of sultry Jupiter and the sacred tomb of old Battus; or as many as are the stars, when the night is silent, that watch the secret loves of humankind: to kiss you so many kisses is enough and more for insane Catullus, which the curious could not be able to count nor jinx with a bad tongue.

## ⟞ 8 ⟝

Poor Catullus, stop being a fool, and consider as lost what you see has perished. Once upon a time the suns shone brightly for you, when you kept going wherever the girl was leading you, beloved by us as much as no other girl will be loved. Then when those many pleasant things took place, which you wanted and the girl was not unwilling, truly the suns shone brightly for you. Now she no longer wants you: you also don't be powerless; don't go after a person who runs from you; don't live miserably; but endure with a steadfast mind; hang tough! Good-bye, girl. Already Catullus is being tough. He will not call upon you; he will not ask for you since you are unwilling. But you will be sorry, when you shall be called a nobody. Wretch, away with you! What life waits for you? Who now will come to you? To whom will you appear beautiful? Whom will you now love? Whose will you be said to be? Whom will you kiss? Whose lips will you be biting? But you, Catullus, be strong of mind and hang tough!

## 9

Veranius, out of all of my friends, the three hundred thousand of them, you, standing out to me, have you come home to your household gods and to your brothers of one mind and to your aged mother? You have made it! What happy news for me! I will see you unharmed and I will hear you talking, as is your custom, about the places, deeds and tribes of Spain; and embracing your neck I shall kiss your pleasant face and eyes. O however much there is of happier men, who is more fortunate or happier than I?

## 10

My Varus had led me at leisure out of the Forum to see his love, a hooker, so then suddenly she seemed to me to be, not really inelegant, not uncharming. But as we came there, different conversations fell upon us, among which were: how was Bithynia doing now, in what shape was she keeping herself, and how much profit had come my way. I responded that which was a fact, that there was nothing for the men themselves, nor for the praetors, nor the cohort, so that each could become wealthier, especially since the praetor was a pervert to them, and did not care at all for the cohort. "But certainly nevertheless," they said, "you must have purchased men for your litter, something which is said to be native to that place." I, so that to the girl I could make myself (appear to be) one rather fortunate person, said, "Things did not go so very badly for me that, because a bad province had fallen to me, I was not able to purchase eight straight-backed men." But I had no one here or there who would be able to pick up onto his neck the broken foot of an old couch. At this point, as befitted the rather crude woman, she said, "Please, for me, my Catullus, lend them to me for a little while; for I want to be carried to the temple of Serapis." "Stop," I said to the girl, "that thing which I just said that I had, my mind is escaping me; my companion, that's Gaius Cinna, he made a purchase for himself. But in fact whether it's his or mine, what is it to me? I use (them) as well as if I had made a purchase for myself. But you live poorly, insulting and evil-minded, before whom it is not possible for someone to be careless."

## 11

Furius and Aurelius, comrades of Catullus, whether he will journey to the farthest Indians, where the shore is pounded by the long-resounding eastern wave, whether to the Hyrcanians, or the gentle Arabs, whether to the Sagae, or the arrow-bearing Parthians, or the waters which the seven-throated Nile colors, whether he will go across the high Alps, visiting the monuments of great Caesar, the Gallic Rhine, the horrible sea and the Britons, the furthest people away, prepared at the same time to try all these things, whichever the will of the heaven-dwellers will bring, announce a few not good words to my girl. Let her live with and thrive with her adulterers, whom she holds having embraced three hundred at one time, loving none of them truly, but at the same time bursting the loins of all of them. Let her not look back as before for my love, which through her fault has fallen just like the flower at the meadow's edge, after it has been touched by a plow passing by.

### ⇥12⇤

Marrucinus Asinius, you do not use your left hand well; in joke and drink you lift the napkins of those rather relaxed people. You think this is funny? It escapes you, you fool, how crude and uncharming a thing it is. You don't believe me? Believe Pollio your brother, who wishes your stealing habits to be exchanged for a talent; he's a young man well versed in wit and practical jokes. Therefore, either expect three hundred hendecasyllables or send the napkin back to me, which does not move me by its value; it is a true keepsake of my companion. For Fabullus and Veranius sent me Saetaban napkins from Spain as a gift. It is necessary that I cherish them as I do my little Veranius and Fabullus.

### ⇥13⇤

You will eat well, my Fabullus, with me, in a few days, if the gods favor you, if you shall have brought with you a good and large dinner, not without the dazzling girl and wine and wit and all the laughs; if, I say, you shall have brought these, my charming friend, you will eat well. For the wallet of your Catullus is full of spiders' webs. But on the contrary, you will receive unmixed loves and something more charming and elegant; for I will give you perfume which the Venuses and Cupids have donated to my girl, which, when you will smell it, you will call upon the gods so that they make you completely, my Fabullus, into a nose.

### ⇥22⇤

That Suffenus, Varus, whom you know well, is a man charming and witty and sophisticated, and the same man produces very many verses. I think that ten thousand or more verses have been written out by him, and not, as often happens, onto a palimpsest; royal pages, new books, new spools, red tassels for the cover, ruled with lead, and all evened-out with pumice. When you read these things, that handsome and sophisticated Suffenus becomes a goatherd or a ditch digger. So much does he differ and change. But what are we to think of this? He who just recently seemed to be a jester or in some area rather shrewd, the same man is cruder than the crude dirt, as soon as he touches poetry; and he is never equally as happy as when he writes a poem. He takes such joy in himself and he himself so admires himself. Surely we are all deceived in the same way; there is nobody in whom in some way you could not see a Suffenus. To each person has been assigned their own flaw; but we do not see what is in the knapsack on our back.

## 27

Boy, server of the good old Falernian wine, fill my rather bitter cups as the law of Postumia orders, she, soggier than a soggy grape. But you, waters, destroyers of wine, depart to wherever it pleases you, and sail away to the conservatives. This is a pure, Thyonian wine.

## 31

Sirmio, jewel of the almost-islands and the islands, whichever ones in still (fresh water) lakes and on the vast (salt water) sea either Neptune supports, how happily and how gladly I look upon you, scarcely believing myself that I have left Thynia and the Bithynian fields, and that I am looking at you in safety. O what is a more fortunate situation than when one's cares have been resolved, when the mind puts aside its burden, and weary from foreign labor we come to our household god and we lie down on our desired bed? This is the one thing in exchange for such great labors. Hail, O charming Sirmio and rejoice with your master rejoicing, and you, O lake of Lydian water, laugh whatever there is of laughter in the house.

## 34

In trust to Diana, we are virgin girls and boys: let us, virgin boys and girls, sing of Diana. O you, daughter of Latona, great offspring of that very great Jupiter, you, whom your mother brought forth near the Delian olive tree, so that you could become mistress of the mountains and the flourishing forests and the hidden thickets and the sounding streams: you are called Juno Lucina by grieving women in childbirth; you are called powerful Trivia and Luna with your false light. O goddess in your monthly course, filling out your annual journey, you fill the rustic houses of the farmer with good fruits. May you be sacred by whatever name it pleases you, and, as you have been accustomed to do from ancient times, may you protect with good prosperity the race of Romulus.

## 35

O papyrus, I wish you could tell my friend, the gentle poet Caecilius, that he should come to Verona, leaving the walls of New Como and the Larian shore. For I wish that he could receive certain thoughts of his friend and mine. Therefore, if he is wise, he will eat up the road although a dazzling girl a thousand times will call him back as he goes or may ask him to delay by throwing both arms around his neck. Now if true things are being reported to me, she is desperate over him with an unconquerable love. For from the time when she read the started Mistress of Didymus, from that time fire consumed the inner marrow of the poor little thing. I sympathize with you, O girl wiser than the Sapphic muse; for the Magna Mater has been charmingly begun by Caecilius.

## 36

Annals of Volusius, waste paper, discharge a vow for my girl. For she made a vow to sacred Venus and Cupid that, if I should be restored to her and would stop flinging my stinging iambs, she would give the choicest writings of the worst poet to the slow-footed god to be burned up with the other useless wood. And so that very bad girl in this way saw that she was vowing to the gods jokingly, charmingly. Now you, created from the blue sea, who dwell in sacred Idalium, and open Urii, and Ancona, and reedy Cnidos, and Amathus, Golgi, and Durrachium, the inn of the Adriatic, grant this vow as received and duly paid, if it is not uncharming and unwitty. But in the meantime, you come into the fire, full of crudity and bad wit, Annals of Volusius, waste paper.

## 43

Hello, girl with not the smallest nose, nor with a nice leg, nor with dark eyes, nor with long fingers, nor with a dry mouth, and with a not too really elegant way of speaking, girlfriend of the bankrupt man from Formio. The province says you are pretty? Our Lesbia is being compared with you? O what an unwise and crude age!

## 44

O our farm, whether Sabine or Tiburtine, for they swear that you are Tiburtine in whom there is no heart to hurt Catullus; but for those who have such heart, they bet anything that you are Sabine. But whether Sabine or more likely Tiburtine, happily I was in your suburban villa, and I expelled from my chest a bad cough, which my stomach gave me, not undeserving, while I was seeking sumptuous meals. For while I was wishing to be a dinner companion of Sestius, I read his speech, "Against the Candidate Antius," full of venom and disease. A frigid cold and nagging cough shook me up to here, until I escaped into your lap and recovered myself through leisure and the nettle. Therefore refreshed, I extend to you the very greatest thanks, because you did not avenge my mistake. No longer do I pray to prevent that, if I shall have received the odious writings of Sestius, their chill shall bring a cold and cough, not upon me, but upon Sestius himself, who then summons me, when I have read his bad book.

## 45

Septimius, holding his love Acme in his lap, says, "My Acme, if I do not love you desperately and am not prepared to love you constantly further throughout all the years, as much as it is possible for someone to love to desperation, may I go by myself alone to meet a green-eyed lion in Libya or scorched India." As he said this, Cupid sneezed approval on the left as before on the right. But Acme, gently bending back her head, kissed the inebriated eyes of the handsome youth with that rosy mouth of hers and said, "Thus, my life, my little Septimius, let us serve only this one master, as the flame of passion burns much greater and much fiercer for me in the soft marrow (of my bones)." As she said this, Cupid sneezed approval on the left as before on the right. Now, having set out from a good omen, they love, are loved with mutual feelings. Poor Septimius prefers Acme alone before all Syrias and Britains: faithful Acme makes her delight and her love in only Septimius. Who has ever seen any luckier people; who has ever seen a more auspicious love?

## 46

Already spring is carrying back a mild warmth; already the fury of the equinoctial sky grows silent because of the pleasant breezes of the west wind. Catullus, the Phrygian fields and the fertile plain of sultry Nicaea must be left. Let us fly to the famous cities of Asia. Already my anxious mind is eager to get wandering; already my happy feet get strong from my eagerness. Farewell sweet groups of companions, whom, far away, having set out from home at the same time, different roads in different ways are carrying back.

## 49

Most eloquent of the descendants of Romulus, as many as there are, and as many as have been, Marcus Tullius, and as many as there will be in other years after, Catullus, the worst poet of all, gives you the greatest thanks; by as much as he is the worst poet of all, so much are you the best patron of all.

## 50

Yesterday, Licinius, at leisure much did we play on my tablets, as we had agreed to be so risqué; each of us writing little verses was playing in meter now this way, now that, returning things mutually through joke and wine. And from there I departed, Licinius, set on fire by your wit and your jokes, such that food could not help miserable me, nor could sleep touch my eyes with its quiet, but overcome by madness, I turned all over the bed, desiring to see the light (of day) so that I could speak with you and be with you right away. But after my half-dead body, wearied by labor, lay on the little bed, this poem, my fine man, I made for you, from which you could perceive my suffering. Now, beware that you be bold; beware, we beg you, that you look down on our prayers, O jewel, (beware) lest Nemesis demand punishment from you. She is a strong-willed goddess; you better watch out against hurting her.

## 51

That man seems to me to be equal to a god; that man, if it is right (to say), seems to go beyond the gods, who sitting opposite, face to face, watches you and hears you sweetly laughing, something which snatches all the senses from poor me; for as soon as I have set my eyes on you, Lesbia, there is nothing left for me; but my tongue gets numb; a gentle flame below my limbs devours me; my ears ring with their own sound; my eyes are covered by twin night. Leisure, Catullus, is a troublesome thing for you; you exult in leisure and too much do you revel in it; leisure destroyed kings and cities that once were happy.

## ⇥ 53 ⇤

I had a laugh recently from the edge of a crowd at someone I do not know, who, when my Calvus had magnificently clarified the Vatinian charges, admiring and raising his hands, he said, "Great gods, an eloquent midget!"

## ⇥ 62 ⇤

It is evening, young men, stand up! Evening from Olympus just finally raises its long-awaited lights. Already it is time to rise up, already (time) to leave sumptuous tables, already the bride will draw near, already the wedding song will be sung. Hymen, Hymenaeus, Hymen, be present, Hymenaeus!

Maidens, do you see the youths? Stand up on the other side; the night-star is showing his eastern fires for sure. So it is sure; do you see how nimbly they have sprung up? Not rashly have they sprung up; they will sing something worthy to surpass. Hymen, Hymenaeus, Hymen, be present, Hymenaeus!

No easy palm (of victory) has been prepared for us, comrades; look how the maidens are practicing the things that have been learned by them. Not in vain do they learn them: they have something which is worth learning; no wonder—they work intensely with their whole mind. We have divided our minds now here, our ears now there; therefore rightly will we be overcome; victory loves care. Therefore, at least now turn your minds back; already they will begin to speak; already it will be proper to respond. Hymen, Hymenaeus, Hymen, be present, Hymenaeus!

O evening-star, what is said to be a crueler fire in the sky? It is you who could be able to tear a daughter away from the embrace of her mother, to tear a clinging daughter away from the embrace of her mother, and to give the chaste girl to a passionate young man. What crueler act could an enemy do in a captured city? Hymen, Hymenaeus, Hymen, be present Hymenaeus!

O evening-star, what shines as a more pleasing light in the sky? It is you who may with your flame confirm the marriage promises which men have made, which their parents before have made, and which they did not join in before your brightness showed itself. What more desirous thing is given by the gods than this fortunate hour? Hymen, Hymenaeus, Hymen, be present, Hymenaeus!

Comrades, the evening-star has taken one girl from us. (NOTE: loss of lines.) For at your arrival always is a guard on watch; at night-time thieves are lurking, whom you, Hesperus (Evening-Star), often catch as you return, the same being but with your name changed to Eous (Morning-Star). But it pleases the maidens to slander you with false complaint. What does it matter if they slander him whom they seek with their silent mind? Hymen, Hymenaeus, Hymen, be present, Hymenaeus!

As a flower is born secretly in enclosed gardens, unknown to the flock, torn by no plow, which the breezes soothe, the sun strengthens, the rain brings forth; many boys, many girls have desired that flower: when the same flower has faded, nipped by a delicate fingernail, no boys, no girls have wanted that flower. Thus as long as a maiden remains untouched, so is she beloved to her kin; when she has lost the chaste flower in her stained body, she does not remain pleasing to boys, nor beloved to girls. Hymen, Hymenaeus, Hymen, be present, Hymenaeus!

As a barren vine, which is born in a bare field, never raises itself up, never brings forth a ripe grape, but bending its tender body with its downward weight, already it touches the top of its shoot with its root; no farmers, no bullocks have cultivated this vine; but if by chance the same vine is joined to a husband elm tree, many farmers and many bullocks have cultivated it; thus as long as a maiden remains untouched, so long does she grow old untilled; when at the mature time she has obtained a proper marriage, she is beloved more to her husband and less worrisome to her father. Hymen, Hymenaeus, Hymen, be present, Hymenaeus!

And you, maiden, do not fight with such a husband. It is not proper to fight the man to whom your father himself has handed you over, your father himself with your mother, whom it is necessary to obey. Your virginity is not totally yours; partially it belongs to your parents; one third part is your father's; one third part has been given to your mother; a third is yours alone: do not fight the two parts who have given to their son-in-law their rights along with the dowry. Hymen, Hymenaeus, Hymen, be present, Hymenaeus!

## 70

My woman says that she prefers to marry no one other than me, not even if Jupiter himself should seek her. That's what she says; but what a woman says to a passionate lover one ought to write in the wind and in fast-moving water.

## 72

Once upon a time, you used to say, O Lesbia, that you knew only Catullus and that you did not wish to hold Jupiter before me. At that time I cherished you not only as a common man would cherish his girlfriend but the way a father cherishes his sons and his sons-in-law. Now I understand you; therefore although I am more vehemently being consumed, nevertheless you are to me much more cheap and more trivial. How is this possible, you ask? Because such an insult compels a lover to be in love more but to have respect less.

## 73

Stop wishing to deserve any thanks from anyone or thinking that someone is able to become loyal; all things are unthanked; it is no profit to have done something well; rather indeed it is wearisome and harmful instead. So it is for me, whom no one angers more seriously or more bitterly than he who just now considered me his one and only friend.

## 75

Lesbia, my mind has been brought down to this point by your fault and my mind itself has so lost itself in its devotion that it is no longer able to wish you well, if you become the very best, nor could it stop loving you if you do all (the bad things).

## 76

If there is any pleasure for a human being recalling earlier good deeds, when he thought that he was loyal, that he had not violated a sacred trust, that by no pact had he abused the power of the gods in order to deceive human beings, then many joys from this ungrateful love are waiting, prepared for you, Catullus, in your long life. For whatever men are able either to say or to do well for someone, these things have been said and done by you. All things which have been entrusted to an ungrateful mind have perished. Therefore why will you all the more torture yourself? Why don't you strengthen yourself in spirit and why don't you lead yourself back, and why don't you stop being miserable since the gods are opposed? It is a difficult thing to quickly set aside a long-existing love; it is difficult, truly you must do this thing by whatever way you can: this is your only salvation, this must be won by you; you must do this, whether it is not possible or is possible. O gods, if it is yours to show mercy, or if to any people you have ever carried final help in death itself, look at poor me; and if I have led my life purely, snatch away this disease and ruin from me, which, creeping into the very bottom of my limbs like a numbness, has expelled joys from my entire heart. No longer do I seek that thing, that she may love me in return, or, what is not possible, that she may wish to be chaste. I myself desire to be healthy and to put down this foul disease. O gods, return this to me in exchange for my loyalty.

## 77

Rufus, whom I, your friend, trusted in vain and to no purpose! In vain? In fact at a great and evil price; is this how you have stolen up to me and burning my inner self you have stolen all my (our) good things, from wretched me? You have stolen them, alas, alas, you are the cruel poison of my life, alas, alas, the disease of our friendship.

## 83

Lesbia says very many bad things to me when her husband is present. This is the greatest joy for that idiot. Hey mule, do you understand nothing? If she were silent, forgetful of us, she would be free from love. Now, because she complains and she talks, not only is she remembering me, but, something that is much more passionate, she is angry; that is, she is being consumed and she talks.

## 84

Arrius was saying "hadvantages" if ever he wanted to say "advantages" and "hambush" if he wanted to say "ambush" and then he hoped that he had spoken marvelously well, whenever he said "hambush" with as much emphasis as possible. I believe that's the way his mother, that's the way his freeborn uncle, that's the way his maternal grandfather and grandmother had spoken. When this man was sent into Syria, the ears of everybody had gotten a rest. They were hearing these same words pronounced gently and softly, and they were not apprehensive about such words afterwards, when suddenly a horrible message is brought that the Ionian waves, after Arrius had gone there, were no longer the Ionian waves but the Hionian waves.

## 85

I hate and I love. Perhaps you ask why am I doing this? I do not know, but I know it is happening and I am being torn in half.

## 86

Quintia is pretty to many people; to me she is dazzling, tall, and well built. These things I will confess thus one by one, but that word totally I deny, pretty. For there is no charm; there is no grain of wit in such a great body. Lesbia is pretty, who is not only wholly the most beautiful but also has alone stolen all the Venuses (beauties, charms, graces) from everybody.

## 87

No woman is able to say that she has been as truly loved as my Lesbia has been loved by me. No loyalty has ever been as great in any pact, as much as has been found from my part in love of you.

## 92

Lesbia always speaks badly to me; nor is she ever quiet about me. May I die if Lesbia does not love me. By what sign? Since things are the same with me: I curse her constantly, but truly may I die if I do not love her.

### ⇥ 95 ⇤

The Zmyrna of my Cinna is finally published, the ninth harvest and ninth winter after it was begun, when in the meantime Hortensius has written five hundred thousand verses . . . The Zmyrna will be sent far to the deep-channeled waters of the Satrachus river; for a long time the white-haired ages will turn over The Zmyrna. But the Annals of Volusius will die at Padua itself, and often will they provide loose tunics for fish.

### ⇥ 95B ⇤

Let the monuments to my heart be small . . . , but let the people take delight in long-winded Antimachus.

### ⇥ 96 ⇤

O Calvus, if something pleasing or acceptable is able to come from our grief to the mute tombs, by which desire we renew old loves and we weep over friendships that once were sent away, certainly untimely death does not cause for Quintilia so much grief as she finds delight in your love.

### ⇥ 101 ⇤

Carried through many nations and through many seas, I am here, brother, at these sad offerings to the dead, so that I might honor you with the final gift of death and so that I might speak in vain to your voiceless ash. From the time when fortune stole you yourself from me, alas! poor brother, improperly stolen from me, now nevertheless in the meantime, accept these things which in the ancient tradition of our parents have been handed down as a sad gift for the burial offerings, soaked very much with the tears of your brother and, brother, forever hail and farewell.

### ⇥ 107 ⇤

If ever something happened to a man desiring and longing and hoping for it, then this is properly pleasing to his mind. And so to us too, this is pleasing, more precious than gold, the fact that you, Lesbia, are restoring yourself to me who desires you. You are restoring yourself to me who desires you but hopes not for you; you yourself are returning yourself to us. O day with a more gleaming mark! Who lives luckier than only me, or who will be able to talk about things that are more to be desired in this life?

### ⇥ 109 ⇤

My life, you promise to me that this love of ours between us would be pleasant and perpetual. Great gods, grant that she may be able to promise truly, and that she speaks this sincerely and from her mind, that it may be possible for us to lead through our whole life this eternal pact of sacred friendship.

# A. P. Latin Lyric Test: Catullus 1–11

Part I: Grammar

### 1

Cui dono lepidum novum libellum
arida modo pumice expolitum?
Corneli, tibi: namque tu solebas
meas esse aliquid putare **nugas**　　　　　　　　　　　　1. Case and reason.
iam tum, cum ausus es unus Italorum　　5
omne aevum tribus explicare cartis
doctis, Iuppiter, et laboriosis.
quare habe tibi quidquid hoc libelli
qualecumque; quod, &lt;o&gt; patrona virgo,
plus uno **maneat** perenne saeclo.　　10　　　　　　　　2. Mood and reason.

### 2

Passer, deliciae meae puellae,
quicum ludere, quem in sinu tenere,
cui primum digitum dare appetenti
et acris solet incitare morsus,
cum desiderio meo nitenti　　5
carum nescio quid lubet iocari,
et solaciolum sui doloris,
credo, ut tum gravis **acquiescat** ardor:　　　　　　　　3. Mood and reason.
tecum ludere sicut ipsa possem
et tristis animi levare curas!　　10

### 2b

tam gratum est mihi quam ferunt **puellae**　　　　　　　4. To whom does this refer?
pernici aureolum fuisse malum,
**quod** zonam soluit diu ligatam.　　　　　　　　　　　5. Antecedent.

### 3

Lugete, O Veneres Cupidinesque,
**et quantum est hominum venustiorum:**　　　　　　　　6. Figure of speech.
passer mortuus est meae puellae,
passer, deliciae meae puellae,
quem plus **illa oculis suis amabat.**　　5　　　　　　　7. Figure of speech.
nam mellitus erat suamque norat
ipsam tam bene quam puella matrem,
nec sese a gremio illius movebat,
**sed circumsiliens modo huc modo illuc**　　　　　　　　8. Scan the line; name
ad solam dominam usque pipiabat;　　10　　　　　　　　　the meter.
qui nunc it per iter tenebricosum
illud, unde negant redire quemquam.
at vobis male sit, malae tenebrae
Orci, quae omnia bella devoratis:
tam bellum **mihi** passerem abstulistis.　　15　　　　　　9. Case and reason.
O factum male! O miselle passer!
**tua nunc opera meae puellae**　　　　　　　　　　　　10. Translate.
**flendo turgiduli rubent ocelli.**

### 4

Phaselus ille, quem videtis, hospites,
ait fuisse navium celerrimus,
neque ullius natantis impetum **trabis**          11. Figure of speech.
nequisse praeterire, sive palmulis
opus foret volare sive linteo.      5
**et hoc negat minacis Hadriatici**          12. Identify in their order of
**negare litus insulasve Cycladas**                  appearance.
Rhodumque nobilem horridamque Thraciam
**Propontida trucemve Ponticum sinum,**
ubi iste post phaselus antea fuit      10
comata silva; nam Cytorio in iugo
loquente saepe sibilum edidit coma.
Amastri Pontica et Cytore buxifer,
**tibi** haec fuisse et esse cognitissima          13. To what does this refer?
ait phaselus: ultima ex origine      15
tuo stetisse dicit in cacumine,
tuo imbuisse palmulas in aequore,
et inde tot per impotentia freta
**erum** tulisse, laeva sive dextera          14. To whom does this refer?
vocaret aura, sive utrumque Iuppiter      20
simul secundus incidisset in pedem;
neque ulla vota litoralibus deis
sibi esse facta, cum veniret a **mari**          15. To what does this refer?
novissimo hunc ad usque limpidum **lacum.**          16. To what does this refer?
sed haec prius fuere: nunc recondita      25
senet quiete seque dedicat tibi,
gemelle Castor et gemelle Castoris.

### 5

**Vivamus**, mea Lesbia, atque amemus,          17. Mood and reason.
rumoresque senum severiorum
omnes unius aestimemus assis!
soles occidere et redire possunt:
nobis cum semel occidit brevis lux,      5
nox est perpetua una dormienda.
da mi basia mille, deinde centum,
dein mille altera, dein secunda centum,
deinde usque altera mille, deinde centum.
dein, cum milia multa fecerimus,      10
conturbabimus illa, ne **sciamus**,          18. Mood and reason.
aut ne quis malus invidere possit,
cum tantum sciat esse basiorum.

### 7

Quaeris, quot mihi basiationes
tuae, Lesbia, sint satis superque.
quam magnus numerus Libyssae harenae
lasarpiciferis iacet Cyrenis
**oraclum** Iovis inter aestuosi     5
et Batti veteris sacrum sepulcrum;
aut quam sidera multa, cum tacet nox,
furtivos hominum vident amores:
tam te **basia** multa **basiare**
vesano satis et super Catullo est,     10
quae nec pernumerare curiosi
possint nec mala fascinare lingua.

19. Figure of speech.

20. Figure of speech.

### 8

Miser Catulle, desinas ineptire,
et quod vides perisse perditum ducas.
fulsere quondam candidi tibi soles,
cum ventitabas quo puella ducebat
amata **nobis** quantum amabitur nulla.     5
ibi illa multa cum iocosa fiebant,
quae tu volebas nec puella nolebat,
fulsere vere candidi tibi soles.
nunc iam illa non volt: tu quoque inpote\<ns noli\>,
nec quae fugit sectare, nec miser vive,     10
sed obstinata mente perfer, obdura.
vale, puella. iam Catullus obdurat,
nec te requiret nec rogabit invitam.
at tu dolebis, cum rogaberis nulla.
scelesta, vae te! quae tibi manet vita?     15
**quis nunc te adibit? cui videberis bella?**
**quem nunc amabis? cuius esse diceris?**
**quem basiabis? cui labella mordebis?**
**at tu, Catulle, destinatus obdura.**

21. Case and reason.

22. Translate.

### 9

Verani, omnibus e meis amicis
antistans mihi **milibus trecentis**,
venistine domum ad tuos penates
fratresque unanimos anumque matrem?
venisti. O mihi nuntii beati!     5
visam te incolumem audiamque Hiberum
narrantem **loca, facta, nationes**,
ut mos est tuus, applicansque collum
iucundum os oculosque suaviabor.
O quantum est hominum beatiorum,     10
quid **me** laetius est beatiusve?

23. Figure of speech.

24. Figure of speech.

25. Case and reason.

## 10

Varus me meus ad suos amores
visum duxerat e foro otiosum,
scortillum, ut mihi tum repente visum est,
**non sane illepidum neque invenustum.**
huc ut venimus, incidere nobis 5
sermones varii, in quibus, quid esset
iam Bithynia, quo modo se haberet,
et quonam mihi **profuisset** aere.
respondi id quod erat, nihil neque ipsis
nec praetoribus esse nec cohorti, 10
cur quisquam caput unctius referret,
praesertim quibus esset irrumator
praetor, nec faceret pili cohortem.
'at certe tamen,' inquiunt 'quod illic
natum dicitur esse, comparasti 15
ad lecticam homines.' ego, ut puellae
unum me **facerem** beatiorem,
'non' inquam 'mihi tam fuit maligne,
ut, provincia quod mala incidisset,
non **possem** octo homines parare rectos.' 20
at mi nullus erat nec hic neque illic,
fractum qui veteris pedem grabati
in collo sibi collocare posset.
hic illa, ut decuit cinaediorem,
'quaeso,' inquit 'mihi, mi Catulle, paulum 25
istos commoda: nam volo ad Serapim
deferri.' 'mane,' inquii puellae,
'istud quod modo dixeram me habere,
**fugit me ratio: meus sodalis—**
**Cinna est Gaius,—is sibi paravit.** 30
**verum, utrum illius an mei, quid ad me?**
utor tam bene quam mihi pararim.
sed tu insulsa male et molesta vivis,
per quam non licet esse neglegentem.'

26. Figure of speech.

27. Mood and reason.

28. Mood and reason.

29. Mood and reason.

30. Translate.

## 11

Furi et Aureli, comites Catulli,
sive in extremos penetrabit Indos,
**litus ut longe resonante Eoa**
 **tunditur unda,**
sive in Hyrcanos Arabasve molles, 5
seu Sagas sagittiferosve Parthos,
sive quae septemgeminus colorat
 aequora Nilus,
sive trans altas gradietur Alpes,
Caesaris visens monimenta magni, 10
Gallicum Rhenum horribile aequor ulti-
 mosque Britannos,
omnia haec, quaecumque feret voluntas
caelitum, temptare simul parati,
pauca nuntiate meae puellae 15
 non bona dicta.
cum **suis vivat valeatque moechis,**
quos simul complexa tenet trecentos,
nullum amans vere, sed identidem omnium
 ilia rumpens; 20
nec meum **respectet**, ut ante, amorem,
**qui** illius culpa cecidit velut prati
ultimi flos, praetereunte postquam
 1tactus **aratro** est.

31. Scan the line; name the meter.
32. Scan and give the special
 name for this line.

33. Figure of speech.

34. Mood and reason.
35. Latin antecedent.

36. Case and reason.

# A. P. Latin Lyric Test: Catullus 1–11

Part II: Free Response Answers

**1**

>soles occidere et redire possunt;
>nobis cum semel occidit brevis lux,
>nox est perpetua una dormienda.

a. Describe the imagery of this passage and explain its significance in relation to the entire poem from which the passage was taken.
b. Describe the course of action that the poet advocates in consequence of the sentiment expressed in the passage.
c. Write out and scan the third line and name the meter.

**2**

>sed obstinata mente perfer, obdura.
>vale, puella. iam Catullus obdurat,
>nec te requiret nec rogabit invitam.
>at tu dolebis, cum rogaberis nulla.
>scelesta, vae te! quae tibi manet vita?
>quis nunc te adibit? cui videberis bella?
>quem nunc amabis? cuius esse diceris?
>quem basiabis? cui labella mordebis?
>at tu, Catulle, destinatus obdura.

a. What is the topic of the poem from which the passage above is taken?
b. Point out three characteristic features of Catullan style in the passage above.
c. How is the reader's perception of the clause *iam Catullus obdurat* (line 2) affected by what is said in the lines that follow?

**3**

>nec sese a gremio illius movebat,
>sed circumsiliens modo huc modo illuc
>ad solam dominam usque pipiabat;
>qui nunc it per iter tenebricosum
>illud, unde negant redire quemquam.

a. (1) To whom or what does *sese* (line 1) refer?
   (2) To whom or what does *illius* (line 1) refer?
b. (1) Give two examples in Latin of sound or metrical effects in the passage above.
   (2) Describe how your examples reinforce the meaning of the passage above.

**4**

> omnia haec, quaecumque feret voluntas
> caelitum, temptare simul parati,
> pauca nuntiate meae puellae
>     non bona dicta.

a. Translate this passage as literally as possible.
b. The words *omnia haec* (line 1) summarize the first three stanzas of this poem. What is the content of these first stanzas?
c. The words *non bona dicta* (line 4) indicate what the content of the last two stanzas of the poem will be. What is the content of the last two stanzas of the poem?
d. Give a reason why the last two stanzas are characterized as *non bona dicta*.

**5**

> nec meum respectet, ut ante, amorem,
> qui illius culpa cecidit velut prati
> ultimi flos, praetereunte postquam
>     tactus aratro est.

In the passage above the poet uses a concrete image to stand for an abstract idea.
a. (1) What is this image?
   (2) What does this image symbolize?
b. Name the meter.
c. Describe the occasion prompting the poem.

**6**

> Passer, deliciae meae puellae,
> quicum ludere, quem in sinu tenere,
> cui primum digitum dare appetenti
> et acris solet incitare morsus,
> cum desiderio meo nitenti                5
> carum nescio quid lubet iocari,
> et solaciolum sui doloris,
> credo, ut tum gravis acquiescat ardor:
> tecum ludere sicut ipsa possem
> et tristis animi levare curas!           10

a. (1) What does the Passer (line 1) represent to the speaker in this poem?
   (2) Write out and translate two Latin words or phrases from the poem and show how each supports your answer to (1).
b. Translate *tecum . . . curas!* (lines 9–10) as literally as possible.
c. Write out and scan line 2 and name the meter.

7
>
> tam gratum est mihi quam ferunt puellae
> pernici aureolum fuisse malum,
> quod zonam soluit diu ligatam.

a. What do we know about the *puella* (*puellae,* line 1) that makes the adjective *pernix* (*pernici,* line 2) appropriate?
b. To what Latin noun does *quod* (line 3) refer?
c. What does the word *zonam* (line 3) symbolize?

8

Varus me meus ad suos amores
visum duxerat e foro otiosum,
scortillum, ut mihi tum repente visum est,
non sane illepidum neque invenustum.
huc ut venimus, incidere nobis    5
sermones varii, in quibus, quid esset
iam Bithynia, quo modo se haberet,
et quonam mihi profuisset aere.
respondi id quod erat, nihil neque ipsis
nec praetoribus esse nec cohorti,    10
cur quisquam caput unctius referret,
praesertim quibus esset irrumator
praetor, nec faceret pili cohortem.
'at certe tamen,' inquiunt 'quod illic
natum dicitur esse, comparasti    15
ad lecticam homines.' ego, ut puellae
unum me facerem beatiorem,
'non' inquam 'mihi tam fuit maligne,
ut, provincia quod mala incidisset,
non possem octo homines parare rectos.'    20
at mi nullus erat nec hic neque illic,
fractum qui veteris pedem grabati
in collo sibi collocare posset.
hic illa, ut decuit cinaediorem,
'quaeso,' inquit 'mihi, mi Catulle, paulum    25
istos commoda: nam volo ad Serapim
deferri.' 'mane,' inquii puellae,
'istud quod modo dixeram me habere,
fugit me ratio: meus sodalis—
Cinna est Gaius,—is sibi paravit.    30
verum, utrum illius an mei, quid ad me?
utor tam bene quam mihi pararim.
sed tu insulsa male et molesta vivis,
per quam non licet esse neglegentem.'

In this poem Catullus depicts a contest of wits between Varus' girlfriend and himself in a vivid and theatrical way. First he sets the stage (lines 1-13), then he presents the dialogue (lines 14-34). In a well-developed essay, discuss the ways in which Catullus develops the characterization of Varus' girlfriend and of himself. You may wish to consider, but are not limited to, such features as setting, word choice, figures of speech, and use of dialogue.

## 9

>Cui dono lepidum novum libellum
>arida modo pumice expolitum?
>Corneli, tibi: namque tu solebas
>meas esse aliquid putare nugas
>iam tum, cum ausus es unus Italorum         5
>omne aevum tribus explicare cartis
>doctis, Iuppiter, et laboriosis.
>quare habe tibi quidquid hoc libelli
>qualecumque; quod, &lt;o&gt; patrona virgo,
>plus uno maneat perenne saeclo.              10

a. In lines 1–2, identify two qualities that Catullus attributes to his poetry. Refer specifically to the text.
b. What contrast or comparison does Catullus draw between his own poetry and the writings of Cornelius Nepos, the addressee (lines 3–7)?
c. How do the words *quod . . . saeclo* (lines 9–10) show that Catullus is being playful in his use of the words *meas nugas*?

## 10

>tam te basia multa basiare
>vesano satis et super Catullo est,
>quae nec pernumerare curiosi
>possint nec mala fascinare lingua.

a. Why does Catullus describe himself as *vesano* (line 2)?
b. To what word in this passage does *quae* (line 3) refer?
c. (1) Name the meter. (2) Write out and scan line 3.

# A. P. Latin Lyric Test: Catullus 12–36

Part I: Grammar

### 12

Marrucine Asini, manu sinistra
non belle **uteris**: in ioco atque vino
tollis lintea neglegentiorum.
hoc salsum esse putas? fugit **te, inepte**:
quamvis sordida res et invenusta est.  5
**non credis mihi? crede Pollioni**
fratri, qui tua furta vel talento
mutari velit: est enim leporum
differtus puer ac facetiarum.
quare aut hendecasyllabos trecentos  10
exspecta, aut mihi linteum remitte,
**quod** me non movet aestimatione,
verum est mnemosynum mei sodalis.
nam sudaria Saetaba ex Hiberis
**miserunt mihi muneri** Fabullus  15
et Veranius: haec **amem** necesse est
ut Veraniolum meum et Fabullum.

1. Explain the form.

2. Figure of speech.

3. Figure of speech.

4. Antecedent in Latin.

5. Figure of speech.
6. Mood and reason.

### 13

Cenabis bene, mi Fabulle, apud me
paucis, si tibi di favent, **diebus,**
si tecum attuleris bonam atque magnam
cenam, **non sine** candida puella
**et vino et sale et omnibus** cachinnis.  5
haec si, inquam, attuleris, venuste noster,
cenabis bene; nam tui Catulli
plenus sacculus est aranearum.
sed contra accipies **meros** amores
seu quid suavius elegantiusve est:  10
**nam unguentum dabo, quod meae puellae**
**donarunt Veneres Cupidinesque,**
**quod tu cum olfacies, deos rogabis,**
**totum ut te faciant, Fabulle, nasum.**

7. Case and reason.

8. Figure of speech.
9. Figure of speech.

10. What is the special meaning here?
11. Translate.

71

### 22

Suffenus iste, Vare, quem probe **nosti**,
homo est **venustus et dicax et urbanus**,
idemque longe plurimos facit versus.
puto esse ego **illi** milia aut decem aut plura
perscripta, nec sic ut fit in palimpseston      5
**relata: cartae regiae, novi libri,
novi umbilici, lora rubra membranae,
derecta plumbo et pumice omnia aequata.**
haec cum legas tu, bellus ille et urbanus
Suffenus unus caprimulgus aut fossor      10
rursus videtur: tantum abhorret ac mutat.
hoc quid **putemus** esse? qui modo scurra
aut si quid hac re scitius videbatur,
idem infaceto est infacetior **rure**,
simul poemata attigit, neque idem umquam  15
aeque est beatus ac poema cum scribit:
tam gaudet in se tamque se ipse miratur.
**nimirum idem omnes fallimur,** neque est quisquam
quem non in aliqua re videre Suffenum
possis. suus cuique attributus est error;      20
sed non videmus manticae quod in tergo est.

### 27

**Minister vetuli puer Falerni,**
inger mi calices amariores,
ut lex Postumiae iubet magistrae
**ebrioso acino ebriosioris.**
at vos quo lubet hinc abite, lymphae,      5
vini pernicies, et ad severos
migrate. hic merus est Thyonianus.

### 31

Paene insularum, Sirmio, insularumque
ocelle, quascumque in liquentibus stagnis
marique vasto fert uterque Neptunus,
quam te libenter quamque laetus inviso,
vix mi ipse credens **Thuniam atque Bithunos**  5
liquisse campos et videre te in tuto.
O quid solutis est beatius curis,
cum **mens onus** reponit, ac peregrino
labore fessi venimus larem ad nostrum,
desideratoque acquiescimus lecto?      10
**hoc est quod unum est pro laboribus tantis.**
salve, O venusta Sirmio, atque **ero** gaude
gaudente, vosque, O Lydiae lacus undae,
ridete quidquid est domi cachinnorum.

### 34

Dianae sumus in fide
puellae et pueri integri:

---

12. Figure of speech.
13. Figure of speech.
14. Case and reason.
15. Discuss the artistry in these lines. Show how the figures of speech contribute to the effectiveness of the passage.
16. Mood and reason.
17. Case and reason.
18. According to Catullus, how are we all deceived a little?

19. Figure of speech.
20. Figure of speech.

21. Figure of speech
22. Figure of speech.
23. Translate.
24. Case and reason.

&lt;Dianam pueri integri&gt;
puellaeque canamus.

O **Latonia,** maximi 5
magna progenies Iovis,
quam mater prope **Deliam**
deposivit olivam,

montium domina ut **fores
silvarumque virentium** 10
**saltuumque reconditorum
amniumque sonantum:**

tu Lucina dolentibus
Iuno dicta puerperis,
tu potens Trivia et notho es 15
dicta lumine Luna.

tu cursu, dea, menstruo
metiens iter annuum,
rustica agricolae bonis
tecta frugibus exples. 20

sis quocumque tibi placet
sancta nomine, Romulique,
antique ut solita es, bona
**sospites** ope gentem.

35
Poetae tenero, meo sodali,
velim Caecilio, papyre, **dicas**
Veronam veniat, Novi relinquens
Comi moenia Lariumque litus.
nam quasdam volo cogitationes 5
**amici** accipiat sui meique.
quare, si sapiet, viam vorabit,
quamvis candida milies puella
euntem revocet, manusque collo
ambas iniciens roget morari. 10
quae nunc, si mihi vera nuntiantur,
illum deperit impotente amore.
nam quo tempore legit incohatam
Dindymi dominam, ex eo misellae
ignes interiorem edunt medullam. 15
ignosco tibi, Sapphica puella
**musa** doctior; est enim venuste
Magna Caecilio incohata Mater.

25. To whom does this refer?

26. To what does this refer?

27. Mood and reason.
28. Figure of speech.

29. Mood and reason.

30. Mood and reason.

31. To whom does this refer?

32. Case and reason.

### 36

Annales Volusi, cacata carta,
votum solvite pro mea puella.
nam sanctae Veneri Cupidinique
vovit, si sibi restitutus essem
desissemque truces vibrare iambos, 5
electissima pessimi poetae
scripta tardipedi **deo** daturam
infelicibus ustulanda lignis.
et hoc **pessima** se puella vidit
iocose lepide vovere divis. 10
nunc o caeruleo **creata** ponto,
quae sanctum Idalium Uriosque apertos
quaeque Ancona Cnidumque harundinosam
colis quaeque Amathunta quaeque Golgos
quaeque Durrachium Hadriae tabernam, 15
acceptum face redditumque votum,
**si non illepidum neque invenustum est.**
at vos interea venite in ignem,
pleni ruris et inficetiarum
annales Volusi, cacata carta. 20

33. To whom does this refer?

34. Case of this word.

35. To whom does this refer?

36. Figure of speech.

# A. P. Latin Lyric Test: Catullus 12–36

Part II: Free Response Answers

**1**

> haec si, inquam, attuleris, venuste noster,
> cenabis bene; nam tui Catulli
> plenus sacculus est aranearum.
> sed contra accipies meros amores
> seu quid suavius elegantiusve est

a. Write out and scan line 1. Name the meter.
b. In *nam . . . aranearum* (lines 2–3), Catullus uses a vivid image to describe his situation. Write out and translate the Latin phrase that contains this image.
c. Translate lines 4–5 as literally as possible.

**2**

> Paene insularum, Sirmio, insularumque
> ocelle, quascumque in liquentibus stagnis
> marique vasto fert uterque Neptunus,
> quam te libenter quamque laetus inviso,
> vix mi ipse credens Thuniam atque Bithunos   5
> liquisse campos et videre te in tuto.
> O quid solutis est beatius curis,
> cum mens onus reponit, ac peregrino
> labore fessi venimus larem ad nostrum,
> desideratoque acquiescimus lecto?            10
> hoc est quod unum est pro laboribus tantis.
> salve, O venusta Sirmio, atque ero gaude
> gaudente, vosque, O Lydiae lacus undae,
> ridete quidquid est domi cachinnorum.

Describe the mood Catullus conveys in the poem above. Cite five specific references to elements in the poem to support your statement.

# A. P. Latin Lyric Test: Catullus 43–53

Part I: Grammar

### 43
Salve, nec minimo puella naso
nec bello pede nec nigris ocellis
nec longis digitis nec ore sicco
nec sane nimis elegante lingua,
decoctoris amica Formiani. 5
ten provincia narrat esse bellam?
tecum Lesbia nostra comparatur?
O saeclum insapiens et infacetum!

1. Translate this poem as literally as possible.

### 44
O funde noster seu Sabine seu Tiburs
(nam te esse Tiburtem autumant, quibus non est
cordi Catullum laedere; at quibus cordi est,
quovis Sabinum pignore esse contendunt),
sed seu Sabine sive verius Tiburs, 5
fui libenter in tua suburbana
villa, malamque pectore expuli tussim,
**non immerenti** quam mihi meus venter,
dum sumptuosas appeto, dedit, cenas.
nam, Sestianus dum volo esse conviva, 10
orationem in Antium petitorem
**plenam veneni et pestilentiae legi.**
hic me gravedo frigida et frequens tussis
quassavit usque, dum in tuum sinum fugi,
et me recuravi **otio**que et urtica. 15
quare refectus maximas tibi grates
ago, meum quod non es ulta peccatum.
nec deprecor iam, si nefaria scripta
Sesti recepso, quin gravedinem et tussim
non mi, sed ipsi Sestio **ferat** frigus, 20
qui tunc vocat me, cum malum librum legi.

2. What is the occasion for this poem?

3. Figure of speech.

4. Figure of speech.

5. Case and reason.

6. Mood and reason.

### 45

Acmen Septimius suos amores
tenens in gremio 'mea' inquit 'Acme,
ni te perdite **amo atque amare** porro
omnes sum assidue paratus annos,
quantum qui pote plurimum perire, 5
solus in Libya Indiaque tosta
caesio veniam obvius leoni.'
hoc ut dixit, Amor sinistra ut ante
dextra sternuit approbationem.
at Acme leviter caput reflectens 10
et dulcis pueri ebrios ocellos
illo purpureo ore suaviata,
'sic,' inquit 'mea vita Septimille,
huic uni domino usque **serviamus**,
ut multo mihi maior acriorque 15
ignis mollibus ardet in medullis.'
hoc ut dixit, Amor sinistra ut ante
dextra sternuit approbationem.
nunc ab auspicio bono profecti
mutuis **animis amant amantur**. 20
unam Septimius misellus Acmen
mavult quam Syrias Britanniasque:
uno in Septimio fidelis Acme
facit delicias libidinesque.
quis ullos homines beatiores 25
vidit, **quis Venerem auspiciatiorem?**

7. Figure of speech.

8. Mood and reason.

9. Name four figures of speech used here.

10. Answer this question.

### 46

Iam ver egelidos refert tepores,
iam caeli furor aequinoctialis
iucundis Zephyri silescit aureis.
**linquantur** Phrygii, Catulle, campi
Nicaeaeque ager uber aestuosae: 5
ad claras Asiae volemus urbes.
iam mens praetrepidans avet vagari,
iam laeti studio pedes vigescunt.
O dulces comitum valete coetus,
longe quos simul a domo profectos 10
diversae varie viae reportant.

11. Mood and reason.

12. Discuss and explain the use of repetition in this poem.

### 49

Disertissime Romuli nepotum,
**quot sunt quotque fuere**, Marce Tulli,
quotque post aliis erunt in annis,
gratias tibi maximas Catullus
agit pessimus omnium poeta, 5
tanto pessimus omnium poeta,
quanto tu optimus omnium patronus.

13. Figure of speech.

14. Explain the occasion and meaning of this poem.

### 50

Hesterno, Licini, die otiosi
multum lusimus in meis tabellis,
ut convenerat esse delicatos:
scribens versiculos uterque nostrum
**ludebat numero modo hoc modo illoc,** 5
reddens mutua per iocum atque vinum.
atque illinc abii tuo lepore
incensus, Licini, facetiisque,
ut nec me miserum cibus **iuvaret**
nec somnus tegeret quiete ocellos, 10
sed toto indomitus furore lecto
versarer, cupiens videre lucem,
ut tecum **loquerer** simulque ut essem.
at defessa labore membra postquam
semimortua lectulo iacebant, 15
hoc, iucunde, tibi poema feci,
ex quo perspiceres meum dolorem.
nunc audax cave sis, precesque nostras,
oramus, cave despuas, ocelle,
ne poenas Nemesis **reposcat** a te. 20
est vemens dea: laedere hanc caveto.

15. Name the meter; scan the line.

16. Mood and reason.

17. Mood and reason.

18. Mood and reason.

### 51

Ille mi par esse deo videtur,
ille, si fas est, superare divos,
**qui sedens adversus identidem te
    spectat et audit**

dulce ridentem, misero quod omnis 5
eripit **sensus** mihi: nam simul te,
Lesbia, aspexi, nihil est super mi
    * * * * * * * * * * * *

lingua sed torpet, tenuis sub artus
flamma demanat, sonitu suopte 10
tintinant aures, **gemina** teguntur
    lumina nocte.

**otium, Catulle, tibi molestum est:
otio exsultas nimiumque gestis:
otium et reges prius et beatas** 15
    **perdidit urbes.**

19. Scan the lines; name the meter.

20. Case of this word.

21. Case of this word.

22. Translate the lines; explain the rationale of these lines and show how they connect with the rest of the poem.

### 53

Risi nescio quem modo e corona,
qui, cum mirifice Vatiniana
meus crimina Calvos explicasset,
admirans ait haec manusque tollens,
'di magni, salaputium disertum!' 5

23. Translate the poem as literally as possible.

# A. P. Latin Lyric Test: Catullus 43–53

Part II: Free Response Answers

**1**

        nunc ab auspicio bono profecti
        mutuis animis amant amantur.
        unam Septimius misellus Acmen
        mavult quam Syrias Britanniasque:
        uno in Septimio fidelis Acme
        facit delicias libidinesque.

Study the above passage. Then, citing specific words or phrases, show how the passage reflects the sentiment, manner of expression, and structure of the poem from which it is drawn.

**2**

        'ni **te** perdite amo atque amare porro
        omnes sum assidue paratus annos,
        quantum qui pote plurimum perire,     5
        solus in Libya Indiaque tosta
        caesio veniam obvius leoni.'

a. Identify the addressee in bold print.
b. Briefly describe the principal idea of the poem from which the passage is taken.

**3**

        hic me gravedo frigida et frequens tussis
        quassavit usque, dum in tuum sinum fugi,
        et me recuravi otioque et urtica.

a. Name the inanimate object addressed in the poem from which this passage is taken.
b. Identify the occasion prompting the poem.
c. Briefly describe the principal idea of the poem.

**4**

> Salve, nec minimo puella naso
> nec bello pede nec nigris ocellis
> nec longis digitis nec ore sicco
> nec sane nimis elegante lingua,
> decoctoris amica Formiani.　　5
> ten provincia narrat esse bellam?
> tecum Lesbia nostra comparatur?
> O saeclum insapiens et infacetum!

In this poem Lesbia is being compared to another woman. Write an essay which explains how Catullus develops the comparison between Lesbia and the other woman. Include such elements as structure, meter, tone, figures of speech, and interesting use of words, and discuss the effect of these elements.

This poem can be read as indirect praise of Lesbia.

a. Write out and translate two Latin phrases in lines 1–4 that suggest a contrast between the *puella* (line 1) and *Lesbia* (line 7).
b. Referring specifically to the Latin, briefly discuss how lines 6–8 reflect Catullus' *urbanitas* (urbane sophistication).

**5**

> gratias tibi maximas Catullus
> agit pessimus omnium poeta,
> tanto pessimus omnium poeta
> quanto tu optimus omnium patronus.

a. To whom does *poeta* (line 2) refer?
b. Translate the first two lines literally.
c. State the name of the *patronus* (line 4).
d. Copy and scan line 4 and name the meter.
e. The poem from which this excerpt is taken has been interpreted as ironical in tone by some and as sincere by others. Choose one of these two interpretations. State your choice and explain how the excerpt supports this interpretation.

**6**

> fui libenter in tua suburbana
> villa, malamque pectore expuli tussim,
> non immerenti quam mihi meus venter,
> dum sumptuosas appeto, dedit, cenas.

a. Translate *fui . . . tussim* (lines 1–2) as literally as possible.
b. The speaker mentions two reasons for his physical problems, one in the passage above, the other elsewhere in the poem. What are the two reasons?

**7**

Iam ver egelidos refert tepores,
iam caeli furor aequinoctialis
iucundis Zephyri silescit aureis.

a. What is the occasion that prompted the poem from which the passage above is taken?
b. What is the poet's mood on this occasion?
c. Describe one noteworthy way in which he expresses it in the poem.
d. Write out and scan line 1, naming the meter.

**8**

atque illinc abii tuo lepore
incensus, Licini, facetiisque,
ut nec me miserum cibus iuvaret
nec somnus tegeret quiete ocellos,
sed toto indomitus furore lecto        5
versarer, cupiens videre lucem,
ut tecum loquerer simulque ut essem.

a. What is the occasion that has caused Catullus to make these remarks?
b. Write out two words or phrases that indicate Catullus' appreciation of Licinius and explain their meanings in the context of this poem.
c. Translate lines 1–4 as literally as possible.

**9**

Iam ver egelidos refert tepores,
iam caeli furor aequinoctialis
iucundis Zephyri silescit aureis.
linquantur Phrygii, Catulle, campi
Nicaeaeque ager uber aestuosae:        5
ad claras Asiae volemus urbes.
iam mens praetrepidans avet vagari,
iam laeti studio pedes vigescunt.
O dulces comitum valete coetus,
longe quos simul a domo profectos      10
diversae varie viae reportant.

In this poem Catullus uses many figures of speech and other stylistic devices characteristic of his work to create and enhance the atmosphere of the poem. Choose two figures of speech and/or stylistic devices, identify them in this poem, and briefly discuss their effect. Be sure to refer to the Latin in the passage above in support of your answer.

**10**

Acmen Septimius suos amores
tenens in gremio 'mea' inquit 'Acme,
ni te perdite amo atque amare porro
omnes sum assidue paratus annos,
quantum qui pote plurimum perire,    5
solus in Libya Indiaque tosta
caesio veniam obvius leoni.'
hoc ut dixit, Amor sinistra ut ante
dextra sternuit approbationem.
at Acme leviter caput reflectens    10
et dulcis pueri ebrios ocellos
illo purpureo ore suaviata,
'sic,' inquit 'mea vita Septimille,
huic uni domino usque serviamus,
ut multo mihi maior acriorque    15
ignis mollibus ardet in medullis.'
hoc ut dixit, Amor sinistra ut ante
dextra sternuit approbationem.
nunc ab auspicio bono profecti
mutuis animis amant amantur.    20
unam Septimius misellus Acmen
mavult quam Syrias Britanniasque:
uno in Septimio fidelis Acme
facit delicias libidinesque.
quis ullos homines beatiores    25
vidit, quis Venerem auspicatiorem?

In the poem above, the lovers try to outdo each other in declaration of love. Throughout the poem, but especially in lines 19–26, the poet conveys his attitude towards the relationship between the young lovers. Compose an essay in which you discuss the poet's attitude and how he conveys it.

# A. P. Latin Lyric Test: Catullus 62

Vesper adest, iuvenes, consurgite: Vesper Olympo
exspectata diu vix tandem lumina tollit.
surgere iam tempus, iam pinguis linquere mensas,
iam veniet virgo, iam dicetur hymenaeus.
Hymen O Hymenaee, Hymen ades O Hymenaee!   5

1. Identify the dominant figure of speech in lines 3–4 and show how it contributes to the poem.

Cernitis, innuptae, iuvenes? consurgite contra;
nimirum Oetaeos ostendit Noctifer ignes.
sic certest; viden ut perniciter exsiluere?
non temere exsiluere, canent quod vincere par est.
Hymen O Hymenaee, Hymen ades O Hymenaee!   10

2. Show by citation from the text two ways in which lines 1–5 and 6–10 may be considered to be paired.

Non **facilis** nobis, aequales, palma parata est;
aspicite, innuptae secum ut meditata requirunt.
non frustra meditantur: habent memorabile quod **sit**;
nec mirum, penitus quae tota mente laborant.
**nos alio mentes, alio divisimus aures;**   15
iure igitur vincemur: **amat victoria curam.**
quare nunc animos saltem convertite vestros;
dicere iam incipient, iam respondere decebit.
Hymen O Hymenaee, Hymen ades O Hymenaee!

3. What word does *facilis* modify?

4. Mood and reason.
5. Name three figures of speech used in line 15.
6. Translate.

Hespere, quis caelo fertur crudelior **ignis**?   20
qui natam **possis** complexu avellere matris,
complexu matris retinentem avellere natam,
et iuveni ardenti castam donare puellam.
quid faciunt hostes capta crudelius urbe?
Hymen O Hymenaee, Hymen ades O Hymenaee!   25

7. Case.
8. Mood and reason.
9. Explain the effect of repetition in lines 21–22.

Hespere, quis caelo lucet **iucundior** ignis?
qui desponsa tua firmes conubia flamma,
quae **pepigere** viri, **pepigerunt** ante parentes,
nec iunxere prius quam se tuus extulit ardor.
quid datur a divis felici **optatius** hora?   30
Hymen O Hymenaee, Hymen ades O Hymenaee!

10. Translate.

11. Figure of speech.

12. Translate.

Hesperus e nobis, aequales, abstulit unam.
* * * * * * * * * * * * * * * * * *
* * * * * * * * * * * * * * * * *
namque tuo adventu vigilat custodia semper,
nocte latent **fures,** quos idem saepe revertens,
Hespere, mutato comprendis nomine Eous.   35
at lubet innuptis ficto te carpere questu.
quid tum, si carpunt, tacita quem mente requirunt?
Hymen O Hymenaee, Hymen ades O Hymenaee!

13. To whom does **fures** refer?

14. What is the subtle duplicity which informs lines 36-37?

Ut flos in saeptis secretus nascitur hortis,
ignotus pecori, nullo convolsus aratro, 40
quem mulcent aurae, firmat sol, educat imber;
multi illum pueri, multae optavere puellae:
idem cum tenui carptus defloruit ungui,
nulli illum pueri, nullae optavere puellae:
sic virgo, dum intacta manet, dum cara suis est; 45
cum castum amisit polluto corpore florem,
nec pueris iucunda manet, nec cara puellis.
Hymen O Hymenaee, Hymen ades O Hymenaee!

Ut vidua in nudo vitis quae nascitur arvo,
numquam **se** extollit, numquam mitem educat uvam, 50
sed tenerum prono deflectens pondere corpus
iam iam contingit summum **radice flagellum**;
hanc nulli agricolae, nulli coluere iuvenci:
at si forte eadem est ulmo coniuncta marito,
**multi illam agricolae, multi coluere iuvenci:** 55
sic virgo, dum intacta manet, dum inculta senescit;
cum par conubium maturo tempore adepta est,
cara viro magis et minus est invisa parenti.
<Hymen O Hymenaee, Hymen ades O Hymenaee!>

Et tu ne pugna cum tali coniuge, virgo.
non aequom est pugnare, pater **cui** tradidit ipse, 60
ipse pater cum matre, **quibus** parere necesse est.
virginitas non tota tua est, ex parte parentum est,
tertia pars patrist, pars est data tertia matri,
tertia sola tua est: noli **pugnare** duobus,
qui **genero** sua iura simul cum dote dederunt. 65
Hymen O Hymenaee, Hymen ades O Hymenaee!

15. Explain carefully how Catullus is using the image of the flower. Be sure your response shows understanding of lines 45–48.

16. To what does *se* refer?

17. Figure of speech.

18. Copy and scan this line.

19. Explain the symbolism of the *vitis* of line 49 as drawn through line 58b.

20. What Latin word is the antecedent?
21. Case and reason.

22. Mood and reason.
23. To whom does this refer?

# A. P. Latin Lyric Test: Catullus 70–109

### 70
Nulli se dicit mulier mea **nubere** malle
  quam mihi, non si se Iuppiter ipse petat.
**dicit: sed mulier cupido quod dicit amanti,**
  **in vento et rapida scribere oportet aqua.**

1. Mood and reason.

2. Translate.

### 72
Dicebas quondam solum te nosse Catullum,
  Lesbia, nec prae me velle tenere Iovem.
dilexi tum te non tantum ut vulgus amicam,
  sed pater ut gnatos diligit et generos.
nunc te cognovi: quare etsi impensius uror,      5
  multo mi tamen es vilior et levior.
qui potis est, inquis? quod amantem iniuria talis
  cogit amare magis, sed bene velle minus.

3. Describe the change in Catullus' feelings.
4. State two figures of speech in this line.
5. Show by example from this poem how Catullus expresses his change of feelings by use of choice or placement of words, shifts of tense and figures of speech.

### 73
Desine de quoquam quicquam bene velle mereri
  aut aliquem fieri posse putare pium.
omnia sunt ingrata, nihil fecisse benigne
  <prodest,> immo etiam taedet obestque magis;
ut mihi, quem nemo gravius nec acerbius urget,      5
  quam modo qui me unum atque unicum amicum habuit.

6. What is the occasion of this poem? Use text references to substantiate your interpretation.
7. Copy and scan line 6. What is the figure of speech and how does that figure of speech add to the pathos of the poem?

### 75
Huc est mens deducta tua mea, Lesbia, **culpa**
  atque ita se officio perdidit ipsa suo,
ut iam nec bene velle **queat** tibi, si optima fias,
  nec desistere amare, omnia si facias.

8. Case.

9. Mood and reason.

### 76
Siqua recordanti benefacta priora voluptas
  est homini, cum se cogitat esse pium,
nec sanctam violasse fidem, nec foedere nullo
  divum ad fallendos numine abusum homines,
multa parata manent in longa aetate, Catulle,      5
  ex hoc ingrato gaudia amore tibi.
nam quaecumque homines bene cuiquam aut dicere possunt
  aut facere, haec a te dictaque factaque sunt.
omnia quae ingratae perierunt credita menti.
  quare iam te cur amplius excrucies?      10
quin tu animo offirmas atque istinc teque reducis,
  et dis invitis desinis esse miser?
difficile est longum subito deponere amorem,
  difficile est, verum hoc qua lubet efficias:
una salus haec est, hoc est tibi pervincendum,      15
  hoc facias, sive id non pote sive pote.
O di, si vestrum est misereri, aut si quibus umquam

10. Using textual references, explain the probable occasion for this poem. Explain the structure of the poem and point out how meter and figures of speech further portray the poet's emotional condition.

extremam iam ipsa in morte tulistis opem,
me miserum aspicite et, si vitam puriter egi,
  eripite hanc pestem perniciemque mihi,  20
quae mihi subrepens imos ut torpor in artus
  expulit ex omni pectore laetitias.
non iam illud quaero, contra me ut diligat illa,
  aut, quod non potis est, esse pudica velit:
ipse valere opto et taetrum hunc deponere morbum.  25
  O di, reddite mi hoc pro pietate mea.

### 77

**Rufe** mihi frustra ac nequiquam credite amice
  (frustra? immo magno cum pretio atque malo),
sicine subrepsti mi, atque intestina perurens
  ei **misero** eripuisti omnia nostra bona?
eripuisti, heu heu nostrae crudele venenum  5
  vitae, heu heu nostrae pestis amicitiae.

11. To whom does this refer?

12. Case and reason.

### 83

Lesbia mi praesente **viro** mala plurima dicit:
  haec illi fatuo maxima laetitia est.
mule, nihil sentis? si nostri oblita taceret,
  sana esset: nunc quod gannit et obloquitur,
non solum meminit, sed, quae multo acrior est res,  5
  irata est.  hoc est, uritur et loquitur.

13. Case and reason.

14. What does Catullus seek to explain by this poem?

### 84

Chommoda dicebat, si quando commoda vellet
  dicere, et insidias Arrius hinsidias,
et tum mirifice sperabat se esse locutum,
  cum quantum poterat dixerat hinsidias.
credo, sic mater, sic liber avunculus eius,  5
  sic maternus avus dixerat atque avia.
hoc misso in Syriam requierant omnibus aures:
  audibant eadem haec leniter et leviter,
nec sibi postilla metuebant talia verba,
  cum subito affertur nuntius horribilis,  10
Ionios fluctus, postquam illuc Arrius isset,
  iam non Ionios esse sed Hionios.

15. This poem has often been interpreted as Catullus' rejection of a phoney life.  Agree or disagree and use widespread citations to support your claim.

### 85

Odi et amo. quare id faciam, fortasse requiris?
  nescio, sed fieri sentio et excrucior.

16. Translate.

### 86

Quintia formosa est multis. mihi candida, longa,
  recta est: haec ego sic singula confiteor.
totum illud formosa nego: nam nulla venustas,
  nulla in tam magno est corpore mica salis.
Lesbia formosa est, quae cum pulcherrima tota est,  5
  tum omnibus una omnis surripuit Veneres.

17. What is it which Catullus is praising in Clodia here?

### 87

**Nulla potest mulier tantum se dicere amatam**
  **vere, quantum a me Lesbia amata mea est.**
nulla **fides** ullo fuit umquam **foedere** tanta,
  quanta in amore tuo ex parte reperta mea est.

18. Translate lines 1 and 2.
19. Define these words; what do they mean to the Roman reader? Why does the speaker use these words?

### 92

Lesbia mi dicit semper male nec tacet umquam
  de me: Lesbia me dispeream nisi amat.
quo signo? quia sunt totidem mea: deprecor illam
  assidue, verum dispeream nisi amo.

20. Scan lines 3 and 4.

21. Explain the reasoning expressed by these lines.

### 95

Zmyrna mei Cinnae nonam post denique messem
  quam coepta est nonamque edita post hiemem,
milia cum interea quingenta Hortensius uno
  * * * * * * * * * * * * * * * * * * * * * *
Zmyrna cavas Satrachi penitus mittetur ad undas,   5
  Zmyrnam cana diu saecula pervolvent.
at Volusi annales Paduam morientur ad ipsam
  et laxas scombris saepe dabunt tunicas.

22. In a few sentences summarize the point of this poem.

### 95b

Parva mei mihi sint cordi monimenta . . . ,
  at populus tumido **gaudeat** Antimacho.

23. Mood and reason.

### 96

Si quicquam mutis gratum acceptumve sepulcris
  accidere a nostro, Calve, dolore potest,
quo desiderio veteres renovamus amores
  atque olim missas flemus amicitias,
certe non tanto mors immatura dolori est   5
  **Quintiliae**, quantum gaudet amore tuo

24. To whom does the word refer?

### 101

Multas per gentes et multa per aequora vectus
  advenio has miseras, frater, ad inferias,
ut te postremo **donarem** munere mortis
  et mutam nequiquam alloquerer cinerem.
quandoquidem fortuna **mihi tete** abstulit ipsum,   5
  heu miser indigne frater adempte mihi,
nunc tamen interea haec, prisco quae more parentum
  tradita sunt tristi munere ad inferias,
accipe fraterno multum manantia fletu,
  atque in perpetuum, frater, ave atque vale.   10

25. Mood and reason.
26. Figure of speech.

## 107

Si quicquam cupido optantique obtigit umquam
  insperanti, hoc est gratum animo proprie.
quare hoc est gratum +nobis quoque+ carius auro
  quod te restituis, Lesbia, mi cupido.
restituis cupido atque insperanti, ipsa refers te     5
  nobis. O lucem candidiore nota!
quis me uno vivit felicior, aut magis +hac est
  +optandus vita dicere quis poterit?

27. What is the apparent occasion for this poem?

## 109

Iucundum, mea vita, mihi proponis amorem
  hunc nostrum inter nos perpetuumque fore.
di magni, facite ut **vere promittere possit**,
  atque id sincere dicat et ex animo,
ut liceat nobis tota perducere vita     5
  aeternum hoc sanctae foedus amicitiae.

28. What previous promise is referred to here? Cite two indications of the speaker's doubt about the promise. For each citation translate two Latin words or phrases from the poem in support of your answer.

# Bibliography

The following list of secondary material may be of some additional help to both teachers and students. Students tend to read articles and commentary when readily available, and when such resources are not pitched at too high a level. As a teacher, one must lead gently in these areas, and endeavor to provide a good balance. Students should be encouraged to develop and express their own feelings about the Latin texts they are translating. They should be energized and challenged by what they read in the secondary literature. It is also helpful for them to examine polished translations of Catullus. On the free response section of the A. P. examination, students will be required to produce their own literal translations of prepared text. Their essays may be informed by some familiarity with the contents of this list.

**Translations:**

Copley, Frank O. *Catullus: The Complete Poetry.* Ann Arbor: University of Michigan Press, 1957.
Gregory, Horace. *The Poems of Catullus.* New York: Grove Press, [1956]; orig. ed. 1928.
Martin, Charles. *The Poems of Catullus.* Omaha: University of Nebraska Press, 1979.
Michie, James. *The Poems of Catullus.* London: Harte-Davis, 1969.
Sisson, Charles H. *The Poems of Catullus.* New York: Viking, 1969.
Swanson, Roy Arthur. *Odi et Amo.* New York: Liberal Arts Press, 1959.
Whigham, Peter. *The Poems of Catullus.* Harmondsworth: Penguin Books, 1966.

**Commentaries:**

Fordyce, C. J. *Catullus: A Commentary.* Oxford: Clarendon Press, 1961.
Forsyth, Phyllis Young. *The Poems of Catullus.* Lanham: University Press of America, 1986.
Garrison, Daniel H. *The Student's Catullus.* Norman: University of Oklahoma Press, 1989.
Merrill, Elmer T. *Catullus.* Boston: Ginn, 1893.
Quinn, Kenneth. *Catullus: The Poems.* London: Macmillan, 1970; 2nd ed. 1973.

**Books:**

Adler, Eve. *Catullan Self-Revelation.* New York: Arno Press, 1981.
Crawford, Michael. *The Roman Republic.* Cambridge: Harvard University Press, 1993.
Ferguson, John. *Catullus.* Oxford: Clarendon Press, 1988.
Havelock, E. A. *The Lyric Genius of Catullus.* Oxford: Blackwell, 1939.
Holoka, James P. *Gaius Valerius Catullus: A Systematic Bibliography.* New York: Garland, 1985.
Kenney, E. J. (ed.). *The Cambridge History of Classical Literature:* Volume II, Part 2: *The Late Republic.* Cambridge: Cambridge University Press, 1982.
Lyne, R. O. A. M. *The Latin Love Poets: From Catullus to Horace.* Oxford: Clarendon Press, 1980.
Martin, Charles. *Catullus.* New Haven: Yale University Press, 1992.

Neudling, C. L. *A Prosopography to Catullus.* Oxford: Iowa Studies in Classical Philology, 1955.
Putnam, Michael. *Essays on Latin Lyric, Elegy and Epic.* Princeton: Princeton University Press, 1982.
Quinn, Kenneth. *The Catullan Revolution.* Revised Edition. Cambridge: W. Heffer and Sons, Ltd., 1969.
Quinn, Kenneth. *Catullus: An Interpretation.* New York: Barnes and Noble, 1973.
Quinn, Kenneth (ed.). *Approaches to Catullus.* New York: Barnes and Noble, 1972.
Ross, David O. *Style and Tradition in Catullus.* Cambridge: Harvard University Press, 1969.
Skinner, Marilyn B. *Catullus' Passer: The Arrangement of the Book of Polymetric Poems.* New York: Arno, 1981.
Small, Stuart P. *Catullus: A Reader's Guide to the Poems.* Lanham: University Press of America, 1983.
Wiseman, T. P. *Catullan Questions.* Leicester: Leicester University Press, 1969.
Wiseman, T. P. *Catullus and His World: A Reappraisal.* Cambridge: Cambridge University Press, 1985.

**Articles:** (arranged according to the order of the poems)

**1**
Cairns, F. "Catullus I." *Mnemosyne* 22 (1969) 153–158.
Elder, J. P. "Catullus I: His Poetic Creed and Nepos." *Harvard Studies in Classical Philology* 71 (1966) 143–149.
Singleton, D. "A Note on Catullus' First Poem." *Classical Philology* 67 (1972) 192–196.

**2**
Bishop, J. D. "Catullus 2 and Its Hellenistic Antecedents." *Classical Philology* 61 (1966) 158–167.
Dettmer, H. "Catullus 2B from a Structural Perspective." *Classical World* 78 (1984) 107–110.
Vinson, M. P. "And Baby Makes Three? Parental Imagery in the Lesbia Poems of Catullus." *Classical Journal* 85 (1989–90) 47–53.

**3**
Johnston, M. "Catullus 3 and the Literature of Pets." *Classical World* 23 (1929) 24.

**4**
Coleman, K. M. "The Persona of Catullus' Phaselus." *Greece and Rome* 28 (1981) 68–72.
Griffith, J. C. "Catullus, Poem 4: A Neglected Interpretation Revived." *Phoenix* 37 (1983) 123–128.
Hornsby, R. A. "The Craft of Catullus (Carm. 4)." *American Journal of Philology* 84 (1963) 256–265.
Putnam, M. C. J. "Catullus' Journey (*Carmen* 4)." *Classical Philology* 57 (1962) 10–19.

**5**
Commager, S. "The Structure of Catullus 5." *Classical Journal* 59 (1964) 361–364.

Fredricksmeyer, E. A. "Observations on Catullus 5." *American Journal of Philology* 91 (1970) 431–445.

Grimaldi, W. M. A. "The Lesbia Love Lyrics." *Classical Philology* 60 (1965) 87–95.

Segal, E. "Catullus 5 and 7: A Study in Complementaries." *American Journal of Philology* 89 (1968) 284–301.

## 7

Bertman, S. "Oral Imagery in Catullus 7." *Classical Quarterly* 28 (1978) 477–478.

Moorhouse, A. "Two Adjectives in Catullus VII." *American Journal of Philology* 84 (1963) 417–418.

## 8

Dyson, M. "Catullus 8 and 76." *Classical Quarterly* 23 (1973) 127–143.

Rowland, R. L. "Miser Catulle: An Interpretation of the Eighth Poem of Catullus." *Greece and Rome* 13 (1966) 15–21.

Schmiel, R. "The Structure of Catullus 8: A History of Interpretation." *Classical Journal* 86 (1991) 158–166.

Skinner, M. B. "Catullus VIII: The Comic Amator as Eiron." *Classical Journal* 66 (1971) 298–309.

Swanson, R. A. "The Humor of Catullus VIII." *Classical Journal* 58 (1963) 193–196w.

## 9

Nielson, R. M. "Catullus 9 and 31: The Simple Pleasure." *Ramus* 8 (1979) 165–173.

## 10

Sedgwick, W. B. "Catullus X: A Rambling Commentary." *Greece and Rome* 16 (1947) 108–114.

## 11

Forsyth, P. Y. "The Thematic Unity of Catullus 11." *Classical World* 84 (1991) 457–464.

Mayer, R. "Catullus' Divorce." *Classical Quarterly* 33 (1983) 297–298.

Mulroy, D. "An Interpretation of Catullus 11." *Classical World* 71 (1977) 237–247.

Putnam, M. C. J. "Catullus 11: The Ironies of Integrity." *Ramus* 3 (1974) 70–86.

Scott, R. T. "On Catullus 11." *Classical Philology* 78 (1983) 39–42.

Sweet, D. R. "Catullus 11. A Study in Perspective." *Latomus* 46 (1987) 510–526.

## 13

Bernstein, W. H. "A Sense of Taste. Catullus 13." *Classical Journal* 80 (1985) 127–130.

Case, B. D. "Guess Who's Coming to Dinner: A Note on Catullus 13." *Latomus* 54 (1995) 875–876.

Dettmer, H. "Closure in the Lesbia Polymetra 1–13." *Classical World* 82 (1988–89) 375–377.

Fitts, R. L. "Reflections on Catullus 13." *Classical World* 76 (1982) 41–42.

Helm, J. J. "Poetic Structure and Humor: Catullus 13." *Classical World* 74 (1980–81) 213–217.

Richlin, A. "Systems of Food Imagery in Catullus." *Classical World* 81 (1988) 355–363.

## 22

Frank, T. "Catullus and Horace on Suffenus and Alfenus." *Classical Quarterly* 14 (1920) 160–162.

Putnam, M. C. J. "Catullus 22.13." *Hermes* 96 (1968) 552–558.

## 27

Putnam, M. C. J. "On Catullus 27." *Latomus* 28 (1969) 850–857.

## 31

Nielson, R. M. "Catullus 9 and 31: The Simple Pleasure." *Ramus* 8 (1979) 165–173.

Witke, C. "Verbal Art in Catullus 31." *American Journal of Philology* 93 (1972) 239–251.

## 35

Fisher, J. M. "Catullus 35." *Classical Philology* 66 (1971) 1–5.

Fredricksmeyer, E. A. "Catullus to Caecilius on Good Poetry (c. 35)." *American Journal of Philology* 106 (1985) 213–221.

Khan, H. A. "Catullus 35 and the Things Poetry Can Do to You." *Hermes* 102 (1974) 475–490.

## 36

Clarke, G. W. "The Burning of Books and Catullus XXXVI." *Latomus* 27 (1968) 575–580.

Comfort, H. "An Interpretation of Catullus 36." *Classical Philology* 24 (1929) 176–182.

Townend, G. B. "A Further Point in Catullus' Attack on Volusius." *Greece and Rome* 27 (1980) 134–136.

## 43

Rankin, H. D. "Catullus and the Beauty of Lesbia (Poems 43, 86 and 51)." *Latomus* 35 (1976) 3–11.

## 44

de Angeli, E. A. "A Literary Chill: Catullus 44." *Classical World* 62 (1969) 354–356.

Jones, C. P. "Parody in Catullus 44." *Hermes* 96 (1968) 379–383.

Murley, C. "Was Catullus Present at Sestius' Dinner ?" *Classical Philology* 33 (1938) 206–208.

## 45

Baker, S. "The Irony of Catullus' Septimius and Acme." *Classical Philology* 53 (1958) 110–112.

Frueh, E. "Sinistra Ut Ante Dextra: Reading Catullus 45." *Classical World* 84 (1990) 15–21.

Ross, D. O. "Style and Content in Catullus XLV." *Classical Philology* 60 (1965) 256–259.

Singleton, D. "Form and Irony in Catullus XLV." *Greece and Rome* 18 (1971) 180–187.

Williams, M. F. "Amor's Head-Cold." *Classical Journal* 83 (1988) 128–132.

## 46

Havelock, E. A. "Comment and Conjecture on Catullus: Homer, Catullus and Poe." *Classical World* 36 (1943) 248–249.

Minyard, J. D. "The Best Modern Translations of Catullus." *Classical Bulletin* 61 (1985) 14–21.
Simpson, C. J. and Simpson, B. G. "Catullus 46." *Latomus* 48 (1989) 75–85.

## 49

Fredricksmeyer, E. A. "Catullus 49, Cicero and Caesar." *Classical Philology* 68 (1973) 268–278.
Laughton, E. "Disertissime Romuli Nepotum." *Classical Philology* 65 (1970) 1–7.
Laughton, E. "Catullus 49: An Acknowledgement." *Classical Philology* 66 (1971) 36–37.
Tatum, W. J. "Catullus' Criticism of Cicero in Poem 49." *Transactions of the American Philological Association* 118 (1988) 179–184.
Thomson, D. F. S. "Catullus and Cicero: Poetry and the Criticism of Poetry." *Classical World* 60 (1967) 225–230.

## 50

Burgess, D. L. "Catullus C. 50. The Exchange of Poetry." *American Journal of Philology* 107 (1986) 576–586.
Clack, J. "Otium Tibi Molestum Est: Catullus 50 and 51." *Classical Bulletin* 52 (1976) 50–53.
Scott, W. C. "Catullus and Calvus." *Classical Philology* 64 (1969) 169–173.
Segal, C. P. "Catullan Otiosi: The Lover and the Poet." *Greece and Rome* 17 (1970) 25–31.
Williams, M. F. "Catullus 50 and the Language of Friendship." *Latomus* 47 (1988) 69–73.

## 51

Finamore, J. F. "Catullus 50 and 51: Friendship, Love and Otium." *Classical World* 78 (1984) 11–19.
Fredricksmeyer, E. A. "Catullus 51 and 68. 51–56: An Observation." *Classical Philology* 78 (1983) 42–45.
Itzkowitz, J. B. "On the Last Stanza of Catullus 51." *Latomus* 42 (1983) 129–134.
Jensen, R. C. "Otium, Catulle, Tibi Molestum Est." *Classical Journal* 62 (1967) 363–365.
Wilkinson, L. P. "Ancient and Modern: Catullus LI Again." *Greece and Rome* 21 (1974) 82–85.

## 53

Comfort, H. "The Date of Catullus 53." *Classical Philology* 30 (1935) 74–76.
Garrod, H. W. "Salapantium Disertum." *Classical Quarterly* 8 (1914) 48–49.
MacKay, L. A. "Catullus 53.5." *Classical Review* 47 (1933) 220.

## 62

Fraenkel, E. "Vesper Adest (Catullus LXII)." *Journal of Roman Studies* 45 (1955) 1–8.
Goud, T. E. "Who Speaks the Final Lines ? Catullus 62: Structure and Ritual." *Phoenix* 49 (1995) 23–32.
Kidd, D. A. "Hesperus and Catullus LXII." *Latomus* 33 (1974) 22–33.

## 72

Barsby, J. A. "Rhythmical Factors in Catullus 72, 75 and 85." *Phoenix* 29 (1975) 83–88.
Davis, J. T. "Poetic Counterpoint: Catullus 72." *American Journal of Philology* 92 (1971) 196–201.

## 76

Bishop, J. D. "Catullus 76: Elegy or Epigram?" *Classical Philology* 67 (1972) 293–294.
Moritz, L. A. "Difficile Est Longum Subito Deponere Amorem." *Greece and Rome* 15 (1968) 53–58.
Rubino, C. A. "The Erotic World of Catullus." *Classical World* 68 (1975) 289–298.
Skinner, M. B. "Disease Imagery in Catullus 76: 17–26." *Classical Philology* 82 (1987) 230–233.

## 83

Holoka, J. P. "Self-Delusion in Catullus 83 and 92." *Classical World* 69 (1975) 119–120.
Rockwell, K. A. "Catullus 83.3: Mule, Nihil Sentis." *Classical Journal* 65 (1969) 27.

## 84

Baker, R. J. and Marshall, B. A. "Commoda and Insidiae: Catullus LXXXIV, 1–4." *Classical Philology* 73 (1978) 49–50.
Ramage, E. S. "Note on Catullus' Arrius." *Classical Philology* 54 (1959) 44–45.
Vandiver, E. "Sound Patterns in Catullus 84." *Classical Journal* 85 (1990) 337–340.

## 85

Bishop, J. D. "Catullus 85: Structure, Hellenistic Parallels, and the Topos." *Latomus* 30 (1971) 633–642.

## 95

Noonan, J. D. "Myth, Humor and the Sequence of Thought in Catullus 95." *Classical Journal* 81 (1986) 299–304.
Solodow, Joseph B. "On Catullus 95." *Classical Philology* 82 (1987) 141–145.
Thomson, D. F. S. "Interpretations of Catullus, II: Catullus 95,8, et Laxas Scombris Saepe Dabunt Tunicas." *Phoenix* 18 (1964) 30–36.

## 96

Davis, J. T. "Quo Desiderio: The Structure of Catullus 96." *Hermes* 99 (1971) 297–302.

## 101

Cederstrom, E. "Catullus' Last Gift to His Brother (c. 101)." *Classical World* 75 (1981) 117–118.
Howe, N. P. "The 'Terce Muse' of Catullus 101." *Classical Philology* 69 (1974) 274–276.

## 107

Dettmer, H. "Catullus 107. 7–8." *Classical World* 80 (1987) 371–373.

## 109

McGushin, P. "Catullus' Sanctae Foedus Amicitiae." *Classical Philology* 62 (1967) 85–93.

## Catullan Poems in English

"His great virtue is sincerity. Strong and simple utterance is given to deep feeling, whether love or hate for Lesbia, sorrow for his brother, or rapture over a friend's home-coming; he ranks with Sappho and Shelley among the greatest lyric poets of all time."

—A. M. Duff in *Oxford Classical Dictionary* (1950)

**On Catullus**
    Tell me not what too well I know
    About the bard of Sirmio…
        Yes, in Thalia's son
    Such stains there are…as when a Grace
    Sprinkles another's laughing face
        With nectar, and runs on.
                Walter Savage Landor

**Little Sparrow, Pretty Sparrow**   (cf. Cat. 2)
    Little sparrow, pretty sparrow,
    Darling of my 'winsome marrow,'
    Plaything, playmate, what you will,
    Tiny love, or naughty Phil,
    Tempted, teased, to peck and hop
    On her slender finger top,
    Free to nuzzle and to rest
    In the sweet valley of her breast;
        Her wee, wee comfort in her sorrow's wane,
        When sinks to sleep the fever of her pain….
                Hartley Coleridge

*From* **Upon the Death of His Sparrow**   (cf. Cat. 3)
    Phil, the late dead, the late dead dear,
    O! may no eye distil a tear
    For you once lost, who weep not here!
    Had Lesbia, too-too kind, but known
    This sparrow, she had scorned her own,
    And for this dead which under lies
    Wept out her heart, as well as eyes.
                Robert Herrick

**To Celia**   (cf. Cat. 5)
    Come, my Celia, let us prove,
    While wee can, the sports of love;
    Time will not be ours for ever:
    He, at length, ours goods will sever.
    Spend not then his gifts in vaine.
    Sunnes that set may rise againe:
    But, if once wee lose this light,
    'Tis, with us, perpetuall night.
    Why should wee deferre our joyes?
    Fame and rumor are but toies.
    Cannot wee delude the eyes
    Of a few poore houshold spyes?
    Or his easier eares beguile,
    So removed by our wile?
    'Tis no sinne love's fruit to steale:
    But the sweet thefts to reveale:
    To bee taken, to be seene,
    These have crimes accounted beene.
                Ben Johnson

**My Lute Awake**   (cf. Cat. 8)
    Perchaunce the lye wethered and old
    The wynter nyghtes that are so cold,
    Playnyng in vain unto the mone;
    Thy wisshes then dare not be told
    Care then who lyst, for I have done.

    And then may chaunce the to repent
    The tyme that thou hast lost and spent
    To cause thy lovers sigh and swoune;
    Then shalt thou knowe beaultie but lent,
    And wisshe and want as I have done….
                Sir Thomas Wyatt

**To My Inconstant Mistress**   (cf. Cat. 8)
    When thou, poor excommunicate
    From all the joyes of loves, shall see
    The full reward and glorious fate
    Which my strong faith shall purchase me,
    Then curse thine own inconstancie…

    Then shalt thou weepe, entreat, complaine
    To Love as I did once to thee;
    When all thy teares shall be as vaine
    As mine were then; for thou shalt bee
    Damn'd for thy false apostasie.
                Thomas Carew

---

These poems are collected in *Catullus: Love and Hate. Selected Short Poems*, edited with notes and running vocabularies by Leo M. Kaiser (Wauconda, IL: Bolchazy-Carducci Publishers, 1986).

### The Invitation (cf. Cat. 13)

...Beere small as comfort, dead as charity.
At which amaz'd, and pondring on the food,
How cold it was, and how it child my blood;
I curst the master; and I damn'd the souce;
And swore I'de got the ague of the house.
Well, when to eat thou dost me next desire,
I'le bring a fever; since thou keep'st no fire.

Robert Herrick

### *From* the Sanskrit of Chauras (cf. Cat. 43)

Even now
I love long black eyes that caress like silk,
Ever and ever sad and laughing eyes,
Whose lids make such sweet shadow when they close
It seems another beautiful look of hers;
I love a fresh mouth, ah, a scented mouth,
And curving hair, subtle as smoke,
And light fingers, and laughter of green gems.

Tr. by E. Powys Mathers

### *From* Second Eclogues (cf. Cat. 51)

My muse, what ail's this ardour?
Mine eys be dym, my lyms shake,
My voice is hoarse, my throte scorchte,
My tong to this my roofe cleaves,
My fancy amazde, my thoughtes dull'd,
My harte dot ake, my life faints,
My sowle beginnes to take leave.

Sir Philip Sidney

### Translation of Catullus 72

Thou saidst that I alone thy heart cou'd move
And that for me thou wou'dst abandon Jove.
I love'd thee then, not with a love defil'd,
But as a father loves his only child.
I know thee now, and tho' I fiercelier burn,
Thou art become the object of my scorn.
See what thy falshood gets; I must confess
I love thee more, but I esteem thee less.

William Walsh

### Cymbeline III,v,70 (cf. Cat. 70, 75, 85)

I love and hate her; for she's fair and royal,
And that she hath all courtly parts, more exquisite
Than lady, ladies, woman; from every one
The best she hath, and she, of all compounded,
Outsells them all. I love her therefore; but
Disdaining me and throwing favours on
The low Posthumus slanders so her judgment
That what's else rare is chok'd; and in that point
I will conclude to hate her, nay, indeed,
To be reveng'd upon her.

Shakespeare

### Epilogue to the Way of the World (cf. Cat. 86, 87)

For, as when painters form a matchless face,
They from each fair one catch some different grace,
And shining features in one portrait blend,
To which no single beauty must pretend;
So poets oft do in one piece expose
Whole belles assemblees of coquettes and beaux.

William Congreve

### Frater Ave atque Vale (cf. Cat. 101)

Row us out from Desenzano, to your Sirmione row!
So they row'd, and there we landed—'O venusta Sirmio!'
There to me thro' all the groves of olive in the summer glow,
There beneath the Roman ruin where the purple flowers grow,
Came that 'Ave atque Vale' of the Poet's hopeless woe,
Tenderest of Roman poets nineteen hundred years ago....

Tennyson

# NOTES

# NOTES

# NOTES

# NOTES

**Vergil**

New Affordable Paperback!
# VERGIL'S AENEID
### Books I-VI
Clyde Pharr

- Introduction  • Notes
- Vocabulary  • Appendix

Pharr's acclaimed edition has never been surpassed in quality and utility. Now this excellent text is available as an affordable paperback.    ISBN: 0-86516-272-7

# VERGIL AENEID
### Books I & II
ed. Waldo E. Sweet

**LATIN TEXT
LATIN PARAPHRASE
NOTES FROM SERVIUS**

**TOTAL IMMERSION IN LATIN**

This is a unique textbook: Instead of student's notes in English, there is a paraphrase in easy Latin facing the original to help the students get the "plain meaning" of the author and selected notes from Servius and others in Latin.
ISBN: 0-86516-023-6

# THE ART OF THE AENEID
William Anderson

*"The classic book for English readers of* The Aeneid.*"*
—American Journal of Philology

The book includes examinations of each of the books of *The Aeneid*, extensive notes, suggestions for further reading and a Vergil chronology.    ISBN 0-86516-237-9

# A VERGIL CONCORDANCE
*compiled by* **Henrietta Holm Warwick**
A *Vergil Concordance* will be useful not only to scholars in classical studies but also to teachers of Vergil.
972 pages, 8-1/2 x 11

**Bolchazy-Carducci Publ., Inc.** 1000 Brown St., Wauconda IL, 60084
Email Bolchazy@aol.com; Fax 847-526-2867; Ph. 847-526-4344

# THE WISDOM OF THE ANCIENTS
## ON BUTTONS

Over 300 aphorisms listed in our catalog
call or write for a free copy
Price: $1.25 each    Minimum Order: $20.00

Call us Today

## Through Buttons
### Vivat Lingua Latina

- L7   Ditat Deus. *(Artes Latinae)* **God enriches.**
- L12  Experientia docet. *(Tacitus Artes Latinae)* **Experience teaches.**
- L22  Homo proponit sed Deus disponit. *(Thomas a Kempis? Artes Latinae)* **Man proposes but God disposes.**
- L32  Pro bono publico. *(Anon. Artes Latinae)* **For the public good.**
- L33  Tempus fugit. *(Anon. Artes Latinae)* **Time flies.**
- L36  Mala herba cito crescit. *(Anon. Artes Latinae)* **A weed grows quickly.**
- L43  Suaviter et fortiter. *(Motto Artes Latinae)* **Gently but firmly.**
- L50  Post tenebras lux. *(Anon. Artes Latinae)* **After the darkness comes light.**
- L72  Silent...leges inter arma. *(Cicero Artes Latinae)* **In time of war the laws are silent.**
- L91  Ipsa scientia potestas est. *(Sir Francis Bacon? Artes Latinae)* **Knowledge itself is power.**
- L96  Nemo malus felix. *(Juvenal Artes Latinae)* **No bad man is happy.**
- L111 Spiritus quidem promptus est, caro vero infirma. *(N.T. Artes Latinae)* **The spirit is willing but the flesh is weak.**
- L124 Finis coronat opus. *(Medieval Artes Latinae)* **The end crowns the work.**
- L127 Vincit omnia veritas. *(Anon. Artes Latinae)* **Truth conquers all.**
- L130 Omne initium est difficile. *(Anon. Artes Latinae)* **Every beginning is difficult.**
- L137 Damnant quod non intellegunt. *(Anon. Artes Latinae)* **They condemn what they do not understand.**
- L142 Qui parce seminat, parce et metit. *(N.T. Artes Latinae)* **Who sows sparingly also reaps sparingly.**
- L159 Sol omnibus lucet. *(Petronius Artes Latinae)* **The sun shines upon us all.**
- L160 Puris omnia pura. *(N.T. Artes Latinae)* **To the pure all things are pure.**
- L169 Sic transit gloria mundi. *(Anon. Artes Latinae)* **Thus passes the glory of the world.**
- L183 Repetitio est mater studiorum. *(Anon. Artes Latinae)* **Repetition is the mother of studies.**
- L225 Nemo liber est qui corpori servit. *(Seneca Artes Latinae)* **No one is free who is a slave to his body.**
- L236 Dulce et decorum est pro patria mori. *(Horace Artes Latinae)* **It is sweet and fitting to die for one's country.**
- L240 Qui desiderat pacem praeparet bellum. *(Vegetius Artes Latinae)* **Who wishes peace should prepare for war.**
- L245 Video meliora proboque, deteriora sequor. *(Ovid Artes Latinae)* **I see and approve the better things, (but) I follow the worse ones.**
- L247 Divide et impera. *(Anon. Artes Latinae)* **Divide and rule.**
- L278 Dabit deus his quoque finem. *(Ver. Aen. 1.199)* **God will terminate even these sorrows.**
- L281 Cedant Arma Togae. *(Cicero)* **Let generals defer to civilians.**
- L282 Non Omnis Moriar. *(Horace)* **Not all of me shall die.**

## Through Buttons
### Vivat Lingua Graeca

- G5  πᾶν δένδρον ἀγαθὸν καρποὺς καλοὺς ποιεῖ. *(St. Matthew, VII. 17)* **Every good tree bringeth forth good fruit.**
- G17 Ἀγαπήσεις τὸν πλησίον σου ὡς σαυτόν. *(St. Matthew, XIX. 19)* **Thou shalt love thy neighbor as thyself.**
- G36 Τὸν καλὸν ἀγῶνα ἠγώνισμαι. *(II Timothy, IV. 7)* **I have fought a good fight.**
- G45 Μὴ κρίνετε ἵνα μὴ κριθῆτε. *(St. Matthew, VII. 2)* **Judge not that ye be not judged.**
- G63 Πρὸς κέντρα μὴ λάκτιζε. *(Aeschylus, Agamemnon, 1624)* **Kick not against the pricks.**

Bolchazy-Carducci Publishers, Inc., 1000 Brown St., Unit 101, Wauconda, IL 60084
847/526-4344; Fax: 847/526-2867; E-mail: Bolchazy@aol.com

# This text is a must for:

anyone who
## teaches or reads
# Latin
and/or
## Modern Literature

582 pp. (1936, rpt. 1996), Paperback
ISBN 0-86515-317-0

*[Rose's] book in fact has its value as a dictionary of Latin literature besides that of a history.*
**Times (London) Literary Supplement**

**Again Available in Paperback**

- indispensable reference tool for teachers and students
- unique, affordable, comprehensive edition
- astute and sensitive analysis
- unsurpassed in scholarship and usefulness
- extensive bibliography by Professor E. Courtney
- all authors of pagan and Christian Latin literature including:
  *Augustine, Boethius, Caesar, Catullus, Cicero, Horace, Livy, Lucretius, Martial, Ovid, Plautus, Servius, Terence, Vergil*

This edition provides complete analyses of the most prominent works of Latin literature, setting them in their historical context and alongside their contemporaries, rating their relative importance in their own time and in later periods, and exploring their influence on subsequent literatures and Western civilization.

Each known work is discussed and analyzed in terms of content, chronology, genre, significance, meaning, genetic relationship to other works, ancient and modern scholarship and influence.

## BOLCHAZY-CARDUCCI Publisher's, Inc.

# The Living Voice of Greek and Latin

selections on cassettes read by
STEPHEN G. DAITZ,
ROBERT P. SONKOWSKY

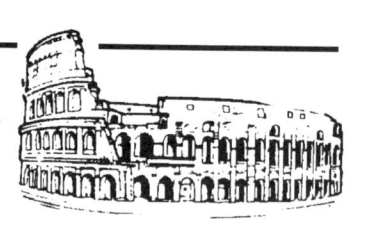

This exciting series of cassette albums for teachers and students features oral performances of important works in Latin by Robert Sonkowsky, Professor of Classics at the University of Minnesota and professional actor, as well as an introductory tape by Professor Stephen Daitz, Professor Emeritus of Classical Languages, City College, CUNY, editor of the series. **The readings incorporate the Restored Classical pronunciation of Latin and Greek after the scholarly conclusions of historical linguistics and endeavour to interpret the selections in accord with the text.** Each recording in this series is produced on clear-sounding cassettes, is housed in a sturdy vinyl album, and is accompanied by the original Latin text and a facing English Translation in booklet form.

> "At last we have something we can put, with all reasonable confidence, into the hands of the student who wants to know what Roman literature sounded like". Gareth Morgan, *Classical World*

### THE PRONUNCIATION AND READING OF CLASSICAL LATIN: A Practical Guide
by **Stephen G. Daitz**

Two cassettes plus an accompanying booklet which contains demonstration texts and practical exercises on **the restored pronunciation** and **the metrics of Latin.** This program explains the pronunciation of the vowels, consonants and dipthongs of classical Latin, the principles of Latin accentuation, and presents a method of reading Latin poetry that integrates the natural word accents with the rhythm based upon syllabic quantity.

**Order #S23675: booklet and 2 cassettes, $34.95**

### VERGIL: Selections
read by **Robert P. Sonkowsky**

Selections from the *Eclogues*, the *Georgics*, and the *Aeneid*.

> "Sonkowsky's fine baritone renders selections from *Aeneid* 1,2,4,6,8,9,11 and 12, *Eclogues* 1,2, and 4, and *Georgics* 4.315-566, totaling three hours. The 5 page preface surveys his intentions: to demonstrate the restored classical pronunciation (on some distinctive features, of which, like nasalized final "m", he comments); and to assign proper value particularly to both accent and quantity as well as the other audible elements of Vergil's art."
> **Edward V. George**, *Classical World*

**Order #S23685: booklet and 2 cassettes, $39.95**

### Read in the Restored Classical Pronunciation of Latin

### CICERO: Selections
read by **Robert P. Sonkowsky**

*In Catilinam I* (complete), *Pro Archia* (complete), selections from other speeches of Cicero, from his rhetorical and philosophical treatises, and from his poetry.

**Order #S23680: booklet and 2 cassettes, $39.95**

### CATULLUS AND HORACE Selections
read by **Robert P. Sonkowsky**

Selections from the poems of Catullus and from the *Odes*, *Epodes* and *Satires* of Horace.

> "Sonkowsky's elegant performance of Catullan and Horatian poetry ought to be essential listening for students and teachers: to hear these poems is to experience them as no purely visual reading allows. ... Sonkowsky offers not just a reading of the poems but truly an interpretation of them through an aural medium, and his performaces enter the critical arena as surely as an interpretive essay..."
> **Victoria Pedrick**, *Classical World*

> "... I can hear Bob Sonkowsky's voice reciting *Integer Vitae*, for my personal and private enjoyment. I can hear the poem, as Horace intended it to be heard...Let me just say that Sonkowsky's reading of Odes 1.22 gives pleasure; that it brings out many possibilities latent in a poem originally written to be read aloud; that good oral renditions may well elicit improved criticism.... Certainly, I feel heartened, listening to Sonkowsky's tape."
> **Kenneth Reckford**, *Arion*

**Order #S23800: booklet and 2 cassettes, $39.95**

Order from:
Bolchazy-Carducci Publishers., Inc.
1000 Brown St., Wauconda IL, 60084, USA;
Email Bolchazy@aol.com;
Fax 847-526-2867; Ph. 847-526-4344

## PROFESSOR ROBERT P. SONKOWSKY on the
# Restored Classical Pronunciation of Latin

Thanks to the progress of scholarship and the development of new approaches to the study of Latin Literature, today we can bring into the classroom two powerful new teaching tools:

1) *The Restored Classical Pronunciation of Latin*
2) *Oral interpretation of Latin Texts based on this pronunciation.*

**The Restored Classical Pronunciation** is very important both for the teaching and learning of Latin. The ancient Classical literatures were oral in their nature and origin. Even after its invention, writing was for centuries used for the storage of texts but very rarely for their silent consumption, since silent reading was almost non-existent. The literatures were composed by ear and for the voice in a living language.

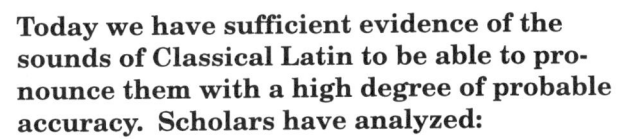

**Today we have sufficient evidence of the sounds of Classical Latin to be able to pronounce them with a high degree of probable accuracy. Scholars have analyzed:**

1. **The statements of the ancients themselves about these sounds,**
2. **Ancient spellings in contemporary stone inscriptions,**
3. **Representations of Latin in other languages,**
4. **Historical developments in the Romance languages,**
5. **Puns and acoustical imitations,**
6. **Internal structural features of the language, including metrics.**

As students and teachers, we are in a position to use the results of this scholarship for the true appreciation of Classical masterpieces.

We must always keep in mind that our goal is to appreciate the aural artistry of the authors. Although we do not have time in our curriculum to do as much with conversational practice as the modern languages, speaking Latin is paradoxically even more important for Latin because of the oral nature of Classical literature.

It is important therefore for Latin teachers today to make the effort to come as close as possible to the generally agreed upon values of the restored sounds in their pronunciation so that a generation of students can be brought up who can produce those sounds. Fortunately, they do not differ in great number from the best traditional American scholastic pronunciation as ideally practiced.

**The most salient difference is the treatment of word-final "m" not as a bilabial hum, but as a sign of nasalization of the preceding vowel.**

In order to master these differences as well as to read aloud in the truly quantitative rhythm of Classical Latin, teachers and students at all levels have, of course, certain habits to overcome. The various discrepancies that exist today are historical and geographic and worthy of study themselves, but the rewards for gaining mastery over them are tremendous.

Along with the other well-known side-benefits of the study of Latin, such as English vocabulary building, students can now acquire experience, skill, and knowledge about their own personal phonetic habits by comparing and contrasting them with Latin. In this way we can extend one of the most solid values of studying Latin, that is to become receptive to aesthetic diversity and the wisdom of diverse cultures.

We can assimilate these restored sounds into our own oral reading or speaking of Latin and make them a part of the oral interpretation of Latin Literature.

I have tried to do this in my recordings of the authors, and I offer them for students to hear, to critique, and, I truly hope, to surpass in their own performances...

**Prof. R. P. Sonkowsky**, *University of Minnesota*

# CICERO'S *PRO CAELIO*
## AP Edition

ed. by
Stephen Ciraolo

The *pro Caelio* is a speech that has great appeal for both the neophyte and the advanced student alike. Perhaps more than any other speech in the corpus, the *pro Caelio* stands out as a *tour de force* of Ciceronian persuasion, but in addition it affords us a privileged view into the social circles haunted by Clodia Metelli, generally assumed to be the notorious Lesbia celebrated in the poetry of Catullus....

Because of its illumination of the Roman society in which Catullus lived and wrote, his friends and their politics and love affairs, it is best read side by side with the poetry of Catullus and when a student first encounters Catullus. Since the committee for the Advanced Placement program in Latin has perceived this and included the *pro Caelio* in the curriculum, a new edition of the speech designed especially for AP students has been badly needed. It is to meet this need that the present edition was undertaken, tested extensively in secondary school and college classes, and now offered to a wider public.

*From the Foreword*
Steven M. Cerutti, Ph.D.
East Carolina University

- Entire text of the speech with emphasis on the AP passages
- Vocabulary and running notes
- Comprehensive vocabulary in the back
- Running stylistic commentary
- Introductory essays

xxxii + 192 pp. (1997), Paperback
ISBN: 0-86516-264-6, $19.00

## BOLCHAZY-CARDUCCI PUBLISHERS, INC.
1000 Brown St., Unit 101, Wauconda, IL 60084
Phone: 847/526-4344 Fax: 847/526-2867; E-mail: "BOLCHAZY@delphi.com"
http://users.aol.com/boochazy/index.html

# Vergil's
# DIDO
## and MIMUS MAGICUS

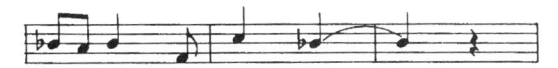

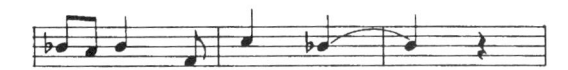

Conducted by **Rafael Kubelik**
Composed by **Jan Novák**

Originally recorded by *audite* Schallplatten, Ostfildern, Germany, 1986.

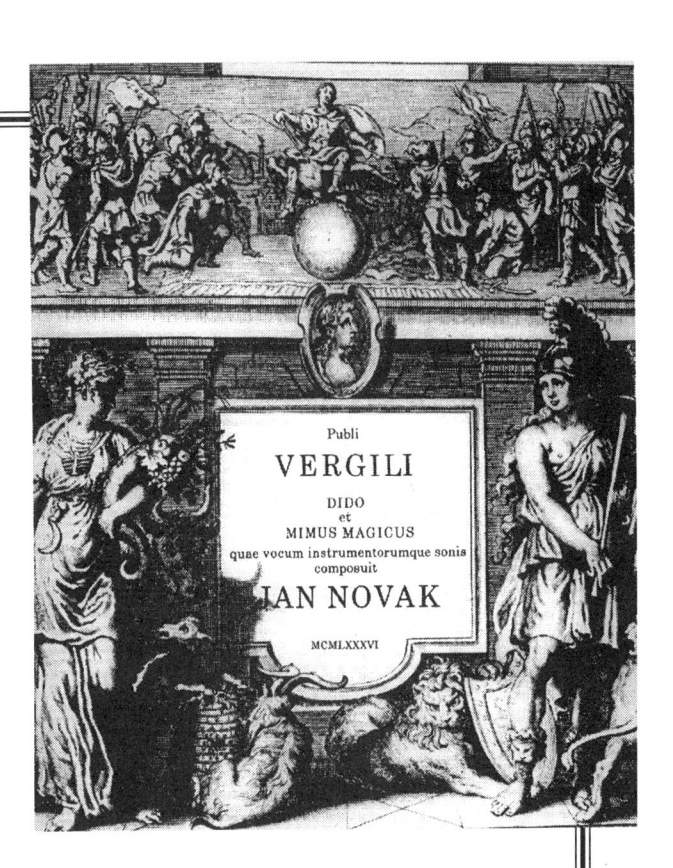

Jan Novák (1921-1984), who is part of the Moravian music tradition represented by composers like Leos Janacek and Bohuslav Martinu, set to music many secular Latin authors of antiquity, the Middle Ages, and modern times.

No other composer ever made the syllable quantities of the Latin language the basis of his work, and with his own special and inimitable ability, Novák brings the rhythm of Latin alive in a very distinctive way.

Now available on CD are Novák's adaptations of two famous Vergil passages: *Dido,* taken from the fourth book of the *Aeneid* and *Mimus Magicus* from Vergil's eighth Eclogue. Both deal with love — but each in its own way!

**The CD comes with a 44-page libretto that contains facing original Latin with German and English translations.**

Limited Edition CD (1997)
44-page libretto in Latin, English and German
ISBN 0-86516-346-4, $30.00

## BOLCHAZY-CARDUCCI PUBLISHERS, INC.
1000 Brown St., Unit 101, Wauconda, IL 60084 USA
Phone: 847/526-4344 Fax: 847/526-2867
E-mail: BOLCHAZY@aol.com; http://users.aol.com/bolchazy/index.html

# Cicero's First Catilinarian Oration

With
Introduction,
Vocabulary,
Notes
Illustrations,
and Maps

## by Karl Frerichs

Cicero's First Catilinarian speech is now available in a practical and inexpensive annotated edition for third-year Latin students. In light of existing textbooks, Karl Frerichs' new edition has several important and distinguished strengths:

- ✦ Clear, tripartite page layout for text, vocabulary and notes on facing pages
- ✦ Running vocabulary separate from notes and complete vocabulary at the end
- ✦ Introduction and *Glossary of Terms and Figures of Speech* provide basic biographical, historical and rhetorical background
- ✦ Maps and illustrations

*Intermediate Level*

80 p., 8 x 11" (1996),
ISBN: 0-86516-341-3, $15.00

**NEW**

"This book's primary purpose is to help make sense of Cicero's Latin without the constant aid of a teacher or a translation. The most important point to remember — and the easiest to forget — is that Cicero meant to be understood."

**K. Frerichs,** *Introduction*

"Karl Frerichs' new commentary on Cicero's **First Catilinarian Oration** is an important contribution to the growing list of Ciceroniana. Students can now read the whole speech with the essential vocabulary and grammar assistance they need."

**Robert W. Cape, Jr.,** From the *Foreword*

"...if the students follow [Frerichs'] advice, they will see the point, understand the situation and the burden placed on Cicero the speaker to deliver a clear, persuasive case to the senators."
**David Conti,** *Polytechnic Preparatory Country Day School,* Brooklyn, NY

"...a perfect text for a third-year high school class or a third-semester college course."
**Deborah McInnes,** *Vanderbilt University*

## BOLCHAZY-CARDUCCI PUBLISHERS, INC.

1000 Brown St., Wauconda, IL 60084, Phone: 847/526-4344, Fax: 847/526-2867
E-mail: **BOLCHAZY@aol.com,** Website: **http://users.aol.com/bolchazy/index.html**